A LIFETIME
OF TRAINING
FOR JUST TEN SECONDS

A LIFETIME OF TRAINING
FOR JUST TEN SECONDS

OLYMPIANS
IN THEIR OWN WORDS

RICHARD WITT

BLOOMSBURY

LONDON · BERLIN · NEW YORK · SYDNEY

In memory of Mike Dempsey, an editor dying young.

Note
Every reasonable effort has been made to trace copyright holders of material
reproduced in this book, but if any have been inadvertently overlooked the
publishers would be glad to hear from them and will correct any omission in
further editions. For legal purposes the list of acknowledgements on page 185
constitutes an extension of the copyright page.

Published by Bloomsbury Publishing Plc
50 Bedford Square
London WC1B 3DP
www.bloomsbury.com

Copyright © Richard Witt 2012

ISBN (print): 978 1 4081 6403 7
ISBN (epub): 978 1 4081 7957 4
ISBN (e-pdf): 978 1 4081 7956 7

A CIP catalogue record for this book is available from the British Library.

Acknowledgements
Opening quote credit www.TheHivesBroadcastingService.com
Front cover quote from Jesse Owens (see page 33).
Cover and text designed by James Watson

This book is produced using paper that is made from wood grown in managed,
sustainable forests. It is natural, renewable and recyclable. The logging and
manufacturing processes conform to the environmental regulations of the
country of origin.

Typeset in 10.5pt Haarlemmer by seagulls.net

Printed and bound in the UK by Clays Ltd

Yes they were smart but they are dead

And you're repeating all that they said

You know it don't make you clever like you thought it would

The Hives, *Dead Quote Olympics*

CONTENTS

PREFACE   ix
1   AMBITION AND BEING THE BEST   1
2   CEREMONIES, SYMBOLS AND INSTITUTIONS   7
3   COTSWOLD, WENLOCK, LONDON   14
4   DESTINY, CHANCE AND THE UNEXPECTED   21
5   DRESS AND FASHION   28
6   ENDURANCE, OPPORTUNITY, WILL AND THE 'IMPOSSIBLE'   32
7   FAIR PLAY, FOUL PLAY AND DOPING   41
8   FAME AND OBLIVION   49
9   FINE ART AND BEAUTY   55
10 FOOD, DRINK AND PARTYING   58
11 DISCIPLINES – GENERAL AND INDIVIDUAL   62
12 MEDALS   72
13 MONEY SPEAKING   81
14 NATIONALISM   91
15 OLYMPIASTADION 1936   98
16 ORIGINS   104
17 OVERCOMING ADVERSITY   107
18 PEOPLE   110
19 POLITICS   125
20 RACIAL DISCRIMINATION   132
21 RELIGION   136
22 REVIVAL   141
23 SEX REARS ITS OLYMPIC HEAD   150
24 TRIUMPH AND DISASTER   153
25 VOICES OF DISSENT   160
26 WAR AND PEACE   164
27 WOMEN'S EMANCIPATION   170
28 YOUTH AND AGE   174
29 THE OLYMPIC HYMN   179
OLYMPIC GAMES: HOST CITIES AND DATES   181
ACKNOWLEDGEMENTS   185
INDEX   187

PREFACE

'O like a book of sport thou'lt read me o'er...'

William Shakespeare, *Troilus and Cressida*

Ni hao, bienvenue, yassou and welcome through the turnstiles to this book of quotations. For me the book is a link in memory to Athens in 2002–2004 when I presided over a gifted team of Olympic translators from Greek into English, and to Beijing in 2000. For you I hope (as a Romford man) the quotes will add a bit of relish to the Games of the XXX Olympiad, held in 2012 in London (where I am glad to have been born).

Are all the quotes in this book genuine? A good question. To illustrate, let us consider the curious incident of the 'Guskos Telegram', which occurred during the first 'modern' Olympics, held in Athens in 1896. Robert Garrett (USA) had just won the shot-put, defeating the favourite, Miltiades Guskos (Greece). Third was Georgios Papasideris (Greece); after him there were three Europeans and another American. Scenting a scoop, an enterprising US journalist dispatched the following artistic telegram to New York, claiming it originated from Garrett: 'Guskos conquered Europe, but I conquered the world.'

Later the journalist's deceit was unmasked. Defiantly unrepentant, and indeed with professional pride, he used the classic defence that although Garrett didn't actually say this, it was *what he would have said*.

This takes us back to fifth-century Greece and the 'father of journalism', the historian Thucydides, who explained how he dealt with people's speeches: 'Some I heard in person. Others I got from this source or that. It being difficult to keep everything in memory, I have consistently made the speakers say what, in my view, was expected from them on any one occasion, sticking as close as possible to their general drift.' His statement of method raises huge questions about how one writes history.

In the pages that follow I've tried to locate and transcribe words exactly as they were spoken, which isn't, sometimes, how they were first transmitted. The fact that a quotation is genuine doesn't necessarily mean it is original. For example: Colin Welland's sports drama film *Chariots of Fire* won four Academy Awards. Its title was lifted from William Blake, who himself had borrowed it from the Old Testament.

A subspecies that I should mention is 'flash quotes'. These are, in theory, blazing words caught from the lips of winning athletes at the finishing line. But in fact they mostly – though not always – sag into tedious, well-worn generalities that a sport writer pressed for time could – and occasionally does – conjure up with ease. Run-of-the-mill journalists and their readers are happiest with stereotyped reactions; and few pole-vaulters are Ernest Hemingway.

Going for gold

'To stop the Duke, go for gold!'

The phrase 'go for gold' is now so much an Olympic cliché that its very origin and the various shifts in meaning it has gone through are somewhat forgotten. The Duke who was to be 'stopped' was Wellington (1769–1852) and this, in 1830, was a slogan used by British activists agitating for constitutional reform; they hoped to start a financial panic by causing a run on the banks' gold reserves. To 'go for' meant here 'to attack'. By contrast, in Australian English 'to go for gold' was, perhaps as early as the 1850s, 'to aim for something higher than your usual (low) standards'. The common denominator is the idea of a target. When American GIs joined them after the Japanese attack on Pearl Harbour in 1941, local gamblers in Hawaii had for some time been using the pidgin phrase 'go for broke' to mean 'bet all one's money on the dice'. (In pidgin, 'brok da mout' – 'breaks the mouth' – is food that is delicious beyond words.) The GIs took 'go for broke' to their hearts, giving the US infantry a combat motto. 'Going for' a supremely important and risky objective became a familiar expression, as in the 1980s management slogan 'go for it'.

What with all the medals involved, 'go for gold' was destined to become an Olympic catchphrase. This happened once the 1980 USA Olympic women's team adopted it as their motto. Bob Hope, in his *Confessions of a [Golf] Hooker* (1985), quipped: 'America is a country where the Olympics and the divorce lawyers both have the same slogan – "Go for the Gold"'.

Duckspeak

The sag and tedium I mentioned earlier are, alas, part and parcel of organising the Games. 'Who can place the least reliance on the so-called Olympic religion's articles of faith?' asked Collectif Anti-Jeux Olympiques (CAJO), the French anti-Olympics caucus, 'written as they are in duckspeak?' If you want to anaesthetise your response to the meanings of words and the nuances of the English language, then apply for a job at the Rio Games.

Like a whale dragging its harpoons, the Olympics advance with their accumulated institutional baggage of technical terms and hallowed clichés. Terms like 'signage' proliferate. A little of the baggage is French, since the Olympic Movement is a last bastion of *Francophonie*. Thus *chef de mission*, the head of a delegation, must never be said in English, though it beats me why not.

Yes, certain terms and phrases are 'Standard', and God shield you from the International Olympic Committee (IOC) if you try and alter them. One is 'Olympic Games': neither word of the two must be omitted, despite the fact that even gold medallists happily refer to 'the Olympics' and that, contradictorily, the useful phrase 'at Games-time' is approved. A 'responsible person', in OlympicSpeak, is not what she or he would be in the real world, 'an individual with a sense of responsibility', but simply the official or minion carrying out a specific function. 'Transportation' – a word that once used to mean 'sending convicts to Australia' – now means, thanks to lobbying by the IOC and others, 'transport'. In the cloud-cuckoo-land of 'facilitating' the 'implementation' of the Games, problems are unthinkable, or at least unthought of; there are only 'issues', which are all, one way or another, 'resolved'.

Pierre Frédy de Coubertin

De Coubertin was born in Paris, 1863. At the age of 19 he visited Rugby School in England and returned to France filled with enthusiasm for the educational possibilities of sport. Patriotic, effusive and hot-tempered, he fought to revive the Olympic Games at Athens in 1896. By tapping into an international network of aristocratic sportsmen, de Coubertin managed to create a self-image for himself as the 'founder of the Olympic movement'. He lived to contribute to and approve of Hitler's 1936 Berlin Games, dying in 1937.

The important thing is...

The idea that what matters is not arriving at a place, but all the things that happen to you while you are still getting there – it is what keeps Homer's *Odyssey* moving, and you can find it in the poetry of Robert Louis Stevenson and Constantine Cavafy for example. In Victorian times, cross-bred with the teachings of St Paul, it resulted in such hymns as Monsell and Boyd's 'Fight the good fight' and in 'improving' literature for boys ('To love the game beyond the prize', Sir Henry Newbolt). It tied in well with the dominant sporting ethos, and as late as 1941 there was a deafening echo of it in US sports writer Grantland Rice's couplet:

> 'And when the One Great Scorer comes to write against your name,
>   He marks, not that you won or lost, but how you played the game.'

Here, the 'Great Scorer' is God's recording angel, and 'the game' is life.

In London in July 1908, after the sixth day of the Games, Britain and the USA were already at each other's throats about sharp practice by athletes, biased judging and assorted postcolonial grievances. Bishop Ethelbert Talbot was deputed to restore peace on Earth with a sermon at a special service for athletes on 19 July. An ex-Bishop of Wyoming in the old days of cattle barons and the six-shooter, he was the right man for the job. What Talbot actually said in the echoing vastness of St Paul's Cathedral (and we have the *Manchester Guardian*'s verbatim report of 22nd July to vouch for it) was:

> '... the lesson of the real Olympia [is] that the Games themselves are better than the race and the prize. St Paul tells us how insignificant is the prize. Our prize is not corruptible, but incorruptible, and though only one may wear the laurel wreath, all may share the equal joy of the contest.'

What Talbot meant was that we should not confuse the short-lived wreath of olive, awarded in the stadium, with the Christian promise of eternal life. In sporting terms, he meant that it is not of the first importance whether the USA or Britain win medals; what matters is goodwill all round.

Below the pulpit in the VIP seats was the self-proclaimed reviver of the Olympic Games – the French baron Pierre Frédy de Coubertin, who could not believe his luck. Whipping out pencil and notebook, one imagines, he jotted down what he saw as the essential relevance of Talbot's 'happy phrasing' to his own cherished Olympism. Less than a week later, on 24th July, and passed through the mangle of his philosophy, his own version made its debut (in French, of course) at an official banquet: 'L' important dans ces Olympiades, c'est moins d'y gagner que d'y prendre part', which translates as 'the important thing in these Olympiads is less to win there, than to take part there'.

It was not quite what Talbot had meant, but it was, like so many of the Baron's borrowings, catchy. Commanding his well-dined audience to cling to his 'stout saying' (his *forte parole*') de Coubertin at once turned it into a general rule ('the basis of a calm and healthy philosophy'). Bits dropped off, and bits were added on. Thus the Baron replaced 'these Olympiads' with 'life', and wrenched a delicately balanced comparison into an absolute commandment by omitting the word 'less'. 'Winning' became 'triumph' and 'taking part' became 'combat', a very different matter. His 'the important thing' was arguably a steal from the Victorian education reformer Matthew Arnold. Finally, transferring the whole caboodle from present to past-perfect, de Coubertin paraphrased his own paraphrase:

'L'important dans la vie ce n'est point le triomphe mais le combat; l'essentiel ce n'est pas d'avoir vaincu mais de s'être bien battu.'
'What is important in life is not the triumph but the context; the essential is not to have won but to have fought well.'

He would modify this formula further, but it was to his original that he reverted when uttering it for the very last time, in a recorded message that was broadcast from Berlin at 5 p.m. on the opening day of the Games on 1st August, 1936.

This phrase would be displayed prominently at future games. In 1948, for example, a large sign at the far end of Wembley Stadium read, line by line, scoreboard-style, in capital letters: 'THE IMPORTANT THING IN/THE OLYMPIC GAMES IS NOT/ WINNING BUT TAKING PART./THE ESSENTIAL THING IN/

LIFE IS NOT CONQUERING /BUT FIGHTING WELL./ BARON DE COUBERTIN'

This was no philosophy for supermen and record-setting victors. Asked by a reporter in 1948 if Greece would win the sailing event, competitor Konstantinos Potamianos said he did not think so; their boats were out of date. 'But after all, does it matter who wins as long as we all do our best?'

So much for the famous quote. But was it good advice? Here, without comment, is the view of Craig Dixon (USA), competitor in the 1948 men's 110m hurdles: 'Well, I wish I'd never seen it, because that made a big impression on me. I thought, "That's right, just being here and competing is the important thing". I had "made it" and I believed I did not have to worry about concentrating. It was a bad influence because I took that message literally.' He came third.

1
AMBITION AND BEING THE BEST

'...καί μοι μάλα πολλ' ἐπέτελλεν Αἰὲν ἀριστεύειν καὶ ὑπείροχον ἔμμεναι ἄλλων.'

'...time and again my father would tell me "Always do your best and be ahead of the others".'

A famous line, in Greek and then translated, from Europe's first epic poem, *The Iliad* of Homer, dating from 730–700 BC, close to the founding of the Games at Olympia in 776 BC. What the poem and the Games have in common is a highly competitive attitude to the battle of life; it is 'good' to 'come first'.

" "

'People could see in me who I am now, an Olympic champ, the best in the world.'

Australian runner Cathy Freeman, after winning the 400m in her home country at Sydney in 2000.

" "

'None was like me in pride of valour, in wrestling, in running, in jumping, in throwing the javelin ... no horse ever bested me in running.'

Digenes Akritas, the hero of eleventh century Greek ballads who guarded the borders of the Byzantine Empire against Arab raiders.

" "

'I guess I might be the best athlete ever.'

An engagingly modest way of putting it. To add to his six gold medals from Athens, in Beijing in 2008 the swimmer Michael Phelps (USA) added eight more: in the butterfly (100m, 200m), freestyle (200m), individual medley (200m, 400m), 4×400m freestyle, 4×100m medley and three relays.

" "

'I run to be known as the greatest runner, the greatest of all time. I could not eat or sleep for a week after I lost in the [1992] Olympics. I have to win or die.'

Future 1500m victor at Atlanta in 1996, Algerian distance runner Noureddine Morceli, disconcerted by the slow pace, finished only seventh in the 1992 final. He was driven by the need to achieve fame – in the service of Allah – and aimed to surpass any runner past or future, including Paavo Nurmi, with his nine Olympic gold medals for distances between 1500 and 10,000 metres (1920–1928), and Emil Zátopek, with his four gold medals in 5000m 10,000m and marathon (1948–1952).

" "

'When I went to a competition ... I would not sit with the other competitors ... and they'd say, why would you do that? I said, because honestly ... I was there to whip your ass. I wasn't there to make friends. Let's have a beer later, after I won. OK?'

African-American athlete Jesse Owens swept to international renown with his four victories at Berlin in 1936 (100m, 200m, 4×100m relay and long jump), leaving Hitler and Goebbels aghast. He was the hero of these Games (said *The Spectator* at the time), and the German fans had 'fallen under his spell'. About competition,

Owens was nothing if not a realist, noting that 'the Indians did not dine with Custer'.

" "

'I declined the invitation to compete in the London Olympics. In those days, I didn't train very much. If I had won the gold medal, I would probably have retired because Olympic gold medals, 1500 metres, there was nothing higher…'

Roger Bannister – later Sir Roger, a distinguished neurologist and Master of Pembroke College, Oxford – was perhaps the finest British athlete never to win an Olympic medal. His only Games was at Helsinki in 1952 where he came fourth; 21 months later he ran the first four-minute mile.

" "

'I really lack the words to compliment myself today.'

Swedish men's figure skater Per Thorén, reflecting immodestly on his 1908 bronze medal.

" "

'You do not boo an Olympic gold medallist. I'm the best in the world. I came here for you. You don't boo me.'

Kurt Angle (USA), 1996 wrestling (100kg) victor, responds to heckles from the crowd at the end of his first World Wrestling Federation major match.

" "

'For athletes, the Olympics are the ultimate test of their worth.'

So thought Mary Lou Retton (USA), 1984 gymnastics all-around victor. The adjective 'ultimate' seems to cling to the Olympics: 'the ultimate, the champions' (Lasse Virén, distance runner), 'the ultimate level of competition' (Russell Mark, marksman), 'the ultimate Olympian' (Steve Redgrave, rower).

" "

'Dream barriers look very high until someone climbs them. Then they are not barriers anymore.'

Lasse Virén (Finland), gold medallist in the men's 5000m and 10,000m in 1972 and again in 1976.

" "

'My ideals of the Olympic Games are all shot. I always imagined it would be a game of heroes. Well, I'm in the semi-finals myself, so it can't be so hot.'

Canadian sprinter Percy Williams went on to win two gold medals in 1928 in the 100m and 200m. Here he talks candidly to his diary on the eve of victory.

" "

'Well, well, well. So I'm supposed to be the world 100 metres champion. (Crushed apples.) No more fun in running now.'

Percy Williams muses – again in his diary in 1928 – on the anticlimax of victory. (In his seventies he would commit suicide with the gun which had been presented to him in recognition of his gold medals.) 'Crushed apples' seems to be his own vivid phrase, not a proverb.

" "

'I wanted to go out on my own terms. It was bizarre, though, because once I stepped down off the podium with my medal, I had no desire to compete [anymore].'

This, at Atlanta in 1996, was the final Olympic gold medal won by American sprinter 'Carl' (Frederick Carlton) Lewis. His nine victories (alongside eight at the World Championships) spanned four Olympiads. Two were for team 4×100m relay (1984, 1996), leaving seven individual golds (long jump in 1984, 1988, 1992 and 1996; 100m in 1984 and 1988; and 200m in 1984).

" "

'I've had it. If anyone sees me near a boat they have my full permission to shoot me.'

British rower Steve (later Sir Steven) Redgrave, victor in five successive Games, in coxed pair, coxed and coxless four (between

1984–2000). The words were taken to indicate his intended retirement after winning his fourth gold medal, in 1996. He competed again in 2000.

" "

'To be honest, I will never have the same hunger again. It's still weird after winning those Olympic golds.'

Athens 2004 saw British distance runner Kelly Holmes reach a career peak, with victories at 800m and 1500m. Here she describes what Steve Redgrave, having won his fifth and last gold medal in 1996, called his 'empty feeling' after 20 years of sustained effort followed by sudden success.

'The Best Games Ever'

Ritually, as each contemporary Olympics closes, the High Priest – more commonly known as the President of the International Olympic Committee (IOC) – announces that the host city has put on 'The Best Games Ever' (TBGE). The assumption, an old-fashioned one, is that day by day (or rather four-year jump by four-year jump), things are getting better and better, despite all appearances to the contrary. For an Olympics not to be declared TBGE, as at Atlanta 1996, is shameful, the IOC's ultimate raspberry.

TBGE, essentially a backward-looking formula, is sometimes optimistically applied to future Games instead: 'That the Olympic Games at Berlin [in 1916] will surpass all previous events of the kind, goes without saying.' But vain was it to prophesy, as Dick Pound did in his *Inside the Olympics* (2004), that at Athens 2004 there would be no financial megalomania, no attempt to outdo Sydney 2000. Like heck there wasn't: for us translators working at Athens the phrase 'the best games ever' came up for translation practically daily. The most sweeping claim yet is by Boris Johnson, mayor of the upcoming host city. His will be 'the best Olympics since they began in 753 BC' – but this is the date of the founding of Rome! Even in AD 160 or so, a Greek writer (Lucian) was referring to 'the most splendid Olympics I have ever seen'.

From 1896 onwards, TBGE is standard fare: 'What with the number of athletes from so many different countries, their quality and their performances, these days obliterated the sporting brilliance of the Olympic Games at Athens in 1896,' declared the report on the 1900 Paris Expo which included the games very much as a sideshow, and without using (except in this one instance) the adjective 'Olympic'.

The idea crops up in many of the relevant official reports that sum up the achievements of each Game. 'The greatest athletic carnival ever held anywhere in the world' (for the 1900 Games); 'The attention of the world at large was far more concentrated on the Games of 1908 than had been the case at any previous celebration' ; 'The London Games of the IV Olympiad … were the biggest success so far'; 'The glorious, sunlit Olympiad of 1912 – the greatest, most important, most brilliant and best-organised athletic festival the world has ever seen' (Stockholm Official Report, piling it on); 'The greatest sporting pageant' (the 1932 Olympics). The journalist Heinz Magerlein lifted it a touch by calling Rome 1960 'the loveliest Games of the modern era', while US team coach Payton Jordan described 1968 as 'the greatest competitive Olympics in history'.

But the variation conceals a core message: the Olympic Games always gets better, just as the Earth is flat and the Moon is made of green cheese. Let nobody accuse the IOC of reckless departure from tradition. It is a relief to hear from an open-minded source: Athens 2004 'was by far the best of all Olympics I've been to', said Carl Lewis.

2
CEREMONIES,
SYMBOLS AND INSTITUTIONS

There are many aspects of the modern Olympic Games that have been added piecemeal over the years, but which are now a firm part of Olympic tradition. The hymn was first sung in 1896. The flag was first hoisted in 1924. The parade of athletes was introduced in 1908. The oaths were first sworn in 1924. The torch (or flame) was first lit in 1928. The three medals were first presented in 1906. The first closing ceremony was in 1956. The village was first constructed in 1924. The programme was first drawn up before all these, in 1895. The mascots became popular only in 1980. Of all these items, only four are genuine reminiscences of ancient times: the hymn, the torch, the parade and the oaths.

" "

'It's more than a game. It's an institution.'

By the time de Coubertin visited Rugby school at the age of only 20, in 1883, he had already read *Tom Brown's Schooldays* (1857), written by the Victorian lawyer and Liberal MP Thomas Hughes, where he had come across this famous description of cricket.

'The modern Games should be exactly the same as the classical Games – naked bodies, tunics, sandals and all – with victory odes and crowns of wild olive.'

Letter to the editor of the Greek newspaper *Asty*, in 1895.

" "

'We should look, gentlemen, not only to the gymnasium at Olympia, but to those tournaments of the Middle Ages, now forgotten or too little known, whose only fault was that they occasionally went beyond what was reasonable in the elegant cult of honour, stoicism and generous conduct.'

De Coubertin, as President of the International Olympic Committee, addressing the guests at the official closing banquet of the 1912 Stockholm Games.

" "

'What a beautiful symbol for men and for Olympism, this relay-race, which becomes reality, a connecting link between the athletes!'

Henri Pouret, the Racecourse Regulations Director for the governing body of French horseracing, *France Galop*, praises the Olympic torch relay in September 1968.

" "

'...ridiculously pretentious guff from a bunch of Greek priestesses...'

The four-yearly lighting of the flame at Ancient Olympia, by buxom Greek maidens of uncertain age doing eurhythmics, is here clobbered by sports writer Simon Barnes.

" "

'Fifteen men abstained from alcohol to fashion the pillar for the Olympic flame at an iron foundry. Night and day they worked ... people came forward for extended shifts.'

Park She-Jik, Chairman of the Committee for Seoul, 1988.

" "

'It will be a stadium of marble that I hope to welcome you to, men of Athens, you and the athletes and strangers who will be our guests.'

Herodes Atticus in AD 138, benevolent governor, Games organiser and city planner, a giant figure in the history of Roman Athens. A latter-day millionaire made and kept a similar promise: Evangelos Averoff-Tositsa, to whom we owe the 1896 Panathenian Stadium in central Athens.

" "

'There wasn't any prancing about with banners and nonsense like that; I suppose we had some kind of Olympic fire, but I don't remember if we did. It was all a splendid lark.'

George (later Sir George) Stuart Robertson, who came third in the 1896 lawn tennis doubles and last in the discus; in later life, he became a QC.

" "

'I've competed in four Olympic Games and they've all done well without big opening ceremonies … And a big no to pop groups…'

Dorothy (Odam-) Tyler MBE, British high jump silver medallist in 1936 and 1948, talking on BBC News in 2008.

" "

'From what I can remember, the opening ceremony was an absolute shambles. We were all late, rushing in, lining up there, higgledy-piggledy.'

British boxing lightweight hopeful Ron Cooper, who competed in London, 1948. This Olympics sometimes overdid the negative reaction against German precision by being a shade slapdash in its organisation.

" "

Team leader (*annoyed*): 'Emil! What are you doing here?'

(*Opening ceremony begins*)

Zátopek (*in a loud whisper*): 'The King George is looking at us. How can I go off now?'

The Czech team leader, worried about his star athlete, had warned the excitable Zátopek not to tire himself out in the hot sun. But Zátopek, determined to watch the opening ceremony, had crept round the back and was trying to hide behind the tallest of the team.

" "

Baillet-Latour (third President of the IOC): 'As host, you must say this sentence: "I declare the Games of the Eleventh Olympiad of the modern era to be open".'

Hitler (*politely*): 'I will make sure, Count, to learn the words by heart.'

In 1935, at Hitler's official reception prior to the Berlin Games. Adolf Hitler was guilty of many things but not here, I think, of irony.

" "

'Dip that flag, and you will be in hospital tonight.'

London 1908, with three burly American-Irish field athletes in a huddle before the opening ceremony. Speaking was hammer thrower Matt McGrath, four times member of the national Olympic squad, who was addressing Martin Sheridan and Ralph Rose.

McGrath was pithily reinforcing Sheridan's earlier advice to Rose, the flagbearer-elect: 'You're the biggest and the strongest. There's no fear of you dropping it [the flag]. But don't think you have to bow and scrape to that bunch in the Royal Box. You carry the Stars and Stripes proudly.'

Many years afterwards (thirty four, to be exact, after Sheridan's death) these conversations were confected into a flash quote, 'This flag dips to no earthly king', bearing the unmistakeable marks of literary invention. What *does* ring true is Sheridan's disclaimer of arrogance ('Ireland has bowed too often, but not any more') at the post-event Press Conference.

" "

'I can help you with that, it's in my suitcase.'

This chance remark at the 1977 IOC banquet solved a 50-year mystery. By 'it', former American athlete Haig 'Harry' Prieste (1896–2001), diving bronze medallist in 1920, meant the long-lost prototype Olympic flag. Presented to the IOC after the 1920 Antwerp closing ceremony, it immediately 'disappeared'. (The finger of suspicion points Prieste's fun-loving team-mate, Duke Kahanamoku.) At Sydney 2000, there was a happy ending, as Prieste was given the opportunity – at the age of 103! – of handing the flag back to its rightful owners at a special ceremony.

" "

'…and on Jove's altar swear without evasion
That he will, absolutely, give no hint
Of fraud in play, or trickery…'

The Athletes' Oath, in Metastasio's *L'Olimpiade* (Venice 1733).

" "

'Nothing I have done professionally will top the feeling I got when singing with John Farnham at the 2000 Olympic Games in Sydney.'

The singer Olivia Newton-John. The composer Richard Strauss, on the other hand, was 'bored stiff' by his work for the Berlin Olympics.

" "

'I thought of the Marseillaise they were going to play for me. It was the finest minute of my life.'

French distance runner Alain Mimoun, Zatopek's great challenger, in 1956 after winning the marathon. Mimoun was second to Zatopek in both the 1948 and the 1952 men's 10,000m, as well as the 1952 marathon.

" "

'Nothing ever will erase that memory, when King Gustav stepped forward to place the gold medal round my neck, while the Stars and Stripes rose to the top of the highest flag pole and the band played "The Star-Spangled Banner".'

Alma Richards (USA), men's high jump victor at Stockholm in 1912. The atmosphere was soured at Rome in 1960 when an already disgruntled Italian public thought the referee wrong in declaring Edward Crook (USA) winner over Tadeusz Walasek (Poland) in the boxing men's middleweight finals. When Crook went up for his medal, seven measured minutes of booing and hissing accompanied the hoisting of the Stars and Stripes and playing of the US anthem. Among the American supporters, singing away at the top of his voice without getting a dime for it, was Bing Crosby.

" "

'The next time they'll get it right'

Cyclist Erika Salumäe (USSR and Estonia), twice 1000m gold medallist (in 1988 and 1992), sighs ruefully at Barcelona 1992 after the officials overseeing the medal ceremony hoisted the Estonian flag upside down. Estonia's previous medal had been in 1936.

" "

'The custom was set of greeting, by the last words spoken on the eve of one Games, the dawning of the next.'

Baron de Coubertin, speaking at the official closing banquet of the Stockholm Games in 1912. And so in what has become almost a tradition in official speeches at the close of the Games, the IOC president both looks back ('this was the best Games ever') and looks forward ('we shall all meet again at the next Games').

" "

'...not like the Olympic Villages you get now...'

Dame Mary Alison Glen Haig, a foil fencer who represented Britain in three Games from 1948 to 1960, compares 1948 with the early twenty-first century.

" "

'All the guys called the Olympic Village a high-class Boy Scout camp.'

Swimmer and film star (as Tarzan), Johnny Weismuller (USA), gold medallist in Paris, 1924 (freestyle: 100m, 400m and 4x200m) and in Amsterdam in 1928 (freestyle: 100m, 4x200m).

" "

'An entire village of bars had sprung up around the stadium, and this village even had its dance halls!'

French hurdler in 1896 and rugby gold medallist in 1900, Frantz 'Obus' Reichel marvels how Olympic entertainments mushroomed at the Paris Expo. In 1960 American coach Ed Temple vainly tried to keep Wilma Rudolph and her buddies away from the Olympic Village Recreation Hall, telling them they hadn't come all the way to Rome to dance.

" "

'It will be an honour to represent my country and get all the kit, stay in the Olympic Village and, when I'm old enough, get a tattoo of the Olympic rings.'

Tom Daley (GB), precocious 10m platform diver, interviewed on Radio 4 in 2008, aged 13.

3
COTSWOLD,
WENLOCK, LONDON

The Games are consciously modelled on people's conception of the classical Olympics and are associated with three places in the British Isles: Chipping Camden in Gloucestershire (seventeenth to nineteenth century), Much Wenlock in Shropshire (nineteenth century) and London (1908, 1948 and 2012).

Chipping Campden

'How they advance true Love, and neighbourhood
And doe both Church and Common-wealth the good…'

Jacobean playwright Ben Jonson in 1636 perceives social benefit in lawyer/entrepreneur Robert Dover's 'Cotswold Games'. These ran successfully at Chipping Campden, Gloucestershire, from 1612 to 1652 (when Puritans stopped play) and from 1660, finally ending in 1852 when they lost their venue owing to parliamentary enclosure of common land.

" "

'As those brave *Grecians* in their happy days,
On Mount *Olympus* to their Hercules
Ordain'd their Games Olympick, and so nam'd:
There then their able youth, leapt, wrestled, ran,
Threw the arm'd dart; and honour'd was the Man
That was Victor ...
Numb'ring their Yeers, still their accounts they made,
Either from this, or that *Olympiade.*
So, Dover, from these Games, by thee begun
Wee'l reckon ours, as time away doth run.'

The organisers will have welcomed English poet Michael Drayton's testimonial in or around the year 1631. Throughout their 240 years, the Cotswold Games' programme included shin-kicking, tug-of-war and obstacle races – not so bizarre if you consider that taekwondo and mountain biking are now Olympic events.

Much Wenlock

In the delightfully sleepy country town of Much Wenlock, on the Welsh Marches, the surgeon William Penny Brookes (1809–1895), local benefactor, Justice of the Peace and social campaigner, founded and presided over an 'Olympian Class', in order 'to promote the moral, physical and intellectual improvement of the inhabitants of the town and neighbourhood'. The class had its own Olympic Games, which the IOC's eighth president Don Juan Samaranch termed 'the inspiration for the modern Olympic movement'. De Coubertin, impressed with the English public-school attitude to sport, visited Brookes, and agreed with him that the Olympic Games must not be an end in itself but must help create a vast programme of universal physical education for young people. In 1890 he wrote:

'If the Olympic Games that Greece has not yet been able to revive still survives today, it is due, not to a Greek, but to Dr William Penny Brookes. It is he who inaugurated them forty years ago, and it is still he, now 82 years old but still alert and vigorous, who continues to organize and inspire them.'

Considering the size of Much Wenlock (with a population of 2,605 ten years ago, according to the 2001 census), the opening ceremony was somewhat spectacular. Wenlock Olympian Society secretary Helen Cromarty writes:

'They came through the town round the Games field, very similar to the opening ceremony of the Olympics today. When Coubertin came to Much Wenlock in 1890 he saw this and loved the pageantry.'

London 1908

The Sportsman encouraged its readers to attend the 1908 Olympics as a once-in-a-lifetime experience, for 'it will be many years before the revived Olympic Games are again held in England'. The main venue was the White City (a name applied to the 1907 Wood Lane Olympic installations because of the pavilions' white marble cladding). The subsidiary venue was Wembley (as yet without its famous football stadium). Having tackled the job 'with commendable efficiency' (to quote Allan Guttmann, US Olympic historian), the National Olympic Committee afterwards issued a book entitled *Replies to Criticisms of the Olympic Games* and it was admitted that 'for some time … the financial outlook had seemed a little black', meaning red.

" "

'As this country is the cradle of athletic sports, it is absolutely essential that the Olympic Games are carried out in a manner worthy of a great athletic nation.'

Balliol man, skilled settler of disputes and 6'5" tall Olympic fencer, runner-up in the 1906 men's épée, William Grenfell, Baron Desborough of Taplow, uttered this vigorous call to action as Organising Committee president in 1908. His many acts of 'fair play' included covering the cost of replacing the USA shooting team's stolen gold medals.

" "

'Seule Londres cependant fit un affichage mural.'

'But only London did a wall poster.'

Henri comte de Baillet-Latour (fourth IOC president) pays London a gracious, rare and well-deserved French compliment in 1908.

London 1948

The morning after the 1948 Games had ended, the achievement of putting them on was summed up by young David Astor, new editor of the English newspaper *The Observer*. Unlike the sports editor of the *Daily Express*, who thought that England would be unable to cope and 'would be jolly well satisfied never to hold the Games again', Astor perceived a success: not the 'glorious landmark' claimed by the Organising Committee's chairman, David Cecil, 6th Marquess of Exeter, a man brought up on imperial greatness, and victor in the 1928 men's 400m hurdles; but something rather different. Despite limited resources, wrote Astor with cool British reserve, the nation had managed to offer a hospitable welcome to great numbers of competitors and visitors from abroad. To our credit, the terraces had been packed, and we had entered a team for every event. All this had been done quietly, 'with none of the nationalistic ostentation which travestied the Olympic spirit in Berlin'.

" "

'But it was wonderful for the country. It was like the sun coming out after the terrible days of war … And we did it on a shoestring … The easy-going atmosphere of the London Games … came as a great relief after the war and provided a true sign that it was all over.'

Dorothy Tyler, MBE, British high jump silver medallist in 1936 and 1948, talking on BBC News in 2008. 'Doing it on a shoestring' (since no one else could afford to) became almost proverbial for the 1948 Games.

" "

'How we ran the Games? Don't ask me! All of London was still bombed. We were still trying to get ourselves going.'

Ron Cooper, boxing lightweight entrant for the 1948 London Games talking on BBC news in 2010. As he noted, one benefit of the Games was that it made work for builders' labourers on the bomb sites dotted all over London.

" "

'The trouble with you British is that you've no sense of publicity. Look, there are no flags, no advertisements, no excitement. Why, in Los Angeles in 1932, we just lived, breathed, thought and slept Olympics. London has just swallowed the Games, like it swallowed the Blitz.'

Exasperated response, blithely ignoring economic realities, of a middle-aged American visitor to the 1948 'Austerity' Games. When the Olympic sailing events were held at Torquay in the far south-west, locals and visitors could not understand why there were so many young people from different countries wandering around. The American's comment, caught up and set down in print by *Observer* journalist William Clark, rings truer than the alleged bar conversation between Denzil Batchelor and a South American visitor (name unknown): 'I am laughing for you. Your weather was like a comedy on English weather … But in all fairness, I am laughing because of your fantastic English runners and jumpers. God bless you English. Always you give the rest of the world something to laugh at.'

" "

Elderly lady (*getting in at Neasden Station*): 'Oh, you're an athlete, aren't you?'

American athlete (*in a tracksuit and carrying a bag, with Bostonian courtliness*): 'Yes, ma'am.'

(*Other passengers smile and nudge one another.*)

Elderly lady: 'Are you competing in the Olympic Games?'

American athlete: 'Yes ma'am, I am.'

Elderly lady: 'What is your event?'

American athlete: 'Eight hundred metres, ma'am.'

Elderly lady: 'How very interesting.'

(*And that's it; three minutes of silence later, she gets off at Willesden Green*).

Overheard on the Bakerloo Line of the London Underground at Games-time. The American athlete was Mal Whitfield, twice victor in the 800m (1948 and 1952).

" "

'At least half of the inhabitants of London had no idea there was an Olympic Games.'

Xavier Frick (Liechtenstein), a versatile athlete who bridged the war years by competing as a middle-distance runner in 1936 and as a cross-country skier in 1948, on the experiences of his small delegation. At one point they lost their way in the City and entered an office full of female secretaries startled at the sudden appearance of three Olympic participants in uniform. Pro-sport as the British are (commented Frick), they seemed more interested in 'the cricket match against Australia' – the 1948 Test series – than in the Olympic Games.

" "

'We didn't do all that jumping about … I can't imagine [us] throwing our caps in the air.'

Yachtsmen have always taken a laid-back view of the Olympics and here David Bond, gold medallist alongside Stewart Morris in the 1948 swallow class, proves no exception.

" "

'I did not do particularly well, but in those days it did not matter. My contemporaries and I had much more fun and a greater sense of achievement than modern athletes do.'

From a personal account posted on the letters page of *The Times*. The correspondent, Thomas Curry, QC, was an Oriel graduate of Oxford, where in autumn 1946 he won the mile, with 17-year-old Roger Bannister finishing as runner-up. In 1948, Curry ran in the 3000m steeplechase.

London 2012

'We are taking home the biggest prize in sport.'

Sir Sebastian Coe, chairman of the London Organising Committee for the Olympic Games and Paralympic Games celebrates the 2012 Olympic Games going to … London!

4
DESTINY, CHANCE
AND THE UNEXPECTED

'We all felt as if the Greek soil had run under the feet of her son to help him on to victory.'

French eyewitness journalist Hughes Le Roux salutes the first marathon victor of all, in 1896, local boy Spyros Louis. Classical Greeks believed that they had defeated the Persians in 480–479 BC because their soil belonged to them and the Persians were there contrary to nature.

" "

'I was not very angry, because I believe in Fate.'

Alain Mimoun, after his defeat in the 10,000m in 1952. Intensely receptive to what he regarded as signals from Fate, he took his losses submissively.

" "

'I knew at age 9 that I wanted to be an Olympic champion.'

Marion Jones, born in 1975, grew up emulating her half-brother's sporting achievements, especially after his early death in 1987. She made her Olympic debut at Sydney, saying that she was 'going for five' gold medals (100m, 200m, long jump and the two relays). She won all five, but returned them retrospectively after confessing to doping.

" "

'That night I sat down with two of my housemates and began dreaming. Suddenly I said: "I'm going to the Olympic Games".'

As a 13-year-old public-schoolboy at Millfield, Duncan Goodhew had 'this fierce feeling [of wanting] to go to the Olympic Games' after being allowed to swim a couple of lengths with British champion Nigel Johnson. At Moscow 1980, Goodhew won gold in the 100m breaststroke.

" "

'...so after the Games were over, I went up to my room, and [on] a little piece of foolscap, I wrote the date on it, September 11th 1976, and on the note I wrote that one day I would run for Canada at the Olympic Games. I didn't want to tell anyone about that dream, because ... people will think it's crazy, but also if we don't achieve it then we'll have to explain why we didn't ... I grew up in an old farmhouse ... and we had wooden floorboards in our house and in my bedroom there were spaces between the floorboards, so I took that note and I folded it up and hid it in the floor.'

Having seen the Montreal Games on her family's small black-and-white TV, 15-year-old Canadian athlete Silvia Ruegger began to examine her technique and her objectives. At the 1984 Los Angeles Games, she finished 8th in the marathon.

" "

Dean of Harvard: 'If you leave before the end of the semester, Connolly, you may not be readmitted.'

James B. Connolly: 'I am *not* resigning and I am *not* making a re-application to enter. But I *am* going to the Olympic Games, so I am through with Harvard right now. Good day, sir.'

Perhaps an apocryphal quote, but Harvard was not the only university to take a dim view of its students competing in distant Athens. James B. Connolly, son of poor Irish-American parents, passed up high school but registered to study classics at Harvard. Deciding, however, that sport brought more glory than scholarship, and disembarking at Athens's port, the Piraeus, barely in time for the 1896 Games, he came first in the triple jump, second in the high jump and third in the long jump. On his return to his home town of Boston, Massachusetts, he received a hero's welcome and a gold watch. In 1948, Harvard offered him as a mark of esteem, an athletic sweater, which he accepted, and a year later an honorary degree, which he refused.

" "

'Raise the level of technique, so that Soviet sportsmen win world supremacy in major sports in the immediate future.'

This edict was issued ahead of the 1952 Helsinki Olympics by the USSR's head of state, Joseph Stalin.

" "

'I knew I had to do it; I knew I would win.'

Australian sprinter Betty Cuthbert is a woman of great religious faith, with a strong sense of destiny. She approached the Tokyo 1964 400m final, which she won, with calm confidence. So had she done for her 100m victory in 1956 at the historic Melbourne venue: 'I broke the tape in 11.5 seconds just like any other race and there seemed nothing special about it.' Her two other gold medals were also at the Melbourne cricket ground (200m and 4×100m relay).

" "

'From the first step, the gun, I knew I had won the race. It was so perfect, right on the money. I coasted over the last three hurdles thinking "It's over, it's over". It's perhaps the only race I ever ran that way.'

Speaking here is the 1968 men's 100m hurdles victor, a bundle of nerves until on the starting-blocks, Willie Davenport (USA). In 1980, he entered as a member of the bobsleigh team, becoming the first African-American competitor ever in the Winter Games.

'I didn't train to make the Olympic team until 1968. I simply trained for the moment. I never even imagined I would be an Olympic athlete. It always seemed to evolve.'

This theory of Olympic success is by courtesy of high jumper Dick Fosbury (USA), 1968 gold medallist, who revolutionised his discipline with his invention of the 'Fosbury Flop'. Others who 'just growed' into Olympic champions were Edwin Moses (USA), 400m hurdles victor in 1976 and 1984 (who had 'no ambition in high school'), and Soviet gymnast Olga Korbut in 1972 (who said 'I wasn't really going to be a star, and overnight I became a star').

" "

'You have to covet the gold medal, and you have to want it more than anyone else. And, you better have a lot of luck!'

Olympian wisdom from Bill Toomey (USA), Mexico City decathlon victor in 1968. New Zealander Peter Snell, 1960 double gold medallist at 800m and 1500m, said that his career 'developed only by lucky circumstances'.

" "

'It was pure accident that Boland was in Greece on holiday and happened to have bought a tennis racket. The purchase was one he would never regret, for this unexpected match won him an Olympic medal.'

From K. Georgiadis's *Olympic Revival* (Ekdotike Athenon, 2003). The programme of the first modern Olympic Games included lawn tennis. Through to the final from the pool stage was Dubliner James Boland, then an undergraduate at Oxford, and a Greek, Dionysios Kasdaglis, son of wealthy entrepreneurs in Egypt.

" "

'If I'm fortunate enough to win next year, I'll keep my mouth shut!'

Even gold medallists are not immune from superstition. Here, in 1999, oarsman Steve Redgrave looks forward to the Sydney Games. His 'luck' held and he added a fifth gold to his existing four.

" "

Chinese husband: 'If my wife is lucky enough to deliver an "Olympic baby", the luck means something more than happiness.'

In China, an Olympic baby was one born at 8.08 a.m. on 8 August 2008. In Chinese belief, eight is the number of perfect felicity.

" "

'The Olympics are always a special competition. It is very difficult to predict what will happen.'

This was the experience of USSR coach and 1988 pole vault gold medallist, the Ukrainian Sergei Bubka. Nevertheless, what won Bubka a Soviet fortune was setting new records, calculating exactly by how little he needed to improve on the previous record.

" "

'Everybody who has been to an Olympics says "expect the unexpected". [Those] kind of psychology games [do] go on … I think it's kind of silly but I'm prepared for it.'

Swimmer Libby Lenton, double Beijing gold medallist in 2008 (100m butterfly and 4×100m medley), defiantly asserting an Australian preference for the rational.

" "

'The reason sport is attractive to many of the general public, not to some intellectuals, is that it's filled with reversals. What you think may happen doesn't happen. A champion is beaten, an unknown becomes a champion, and I had set my mind on winning the 1500m gold medal in Helsinki in 1952.'

Roger Bannister, who came fourth. The gold and bronze went, in a thrilling finish, to two 'outsiders', one of them Barthel of Luxembourg.

" "

'…the surest sure thing of the Games…'

The prediction was by American journalist Jesse Abramson on the eve of the 1948 men's 400m, for the favourite, the USA's Herb McKenley, to win. With less than 20 metres to go, he was caught and passed by Arthur Wint (GB).

'I expect an easy victory.'

Arguably the greatest of Ethiopian athletes, Abebe Bikila had won the Olympic marathon in Rome (shrugging off a spectator riding a moped at the finish), and also the next marathon at Tokyo in 1964. He predicted, over-optimistically as it turned out, a third consecutive victory at Mexico City in 1968. However, running with a broken bone in his foot, he dropped out of the latter race halfway.

" "

'I'm going to win. I've known it all along … I can trim any sprinter who ever lived.'

Loren Murchison (USA), twice victor in the men's 4×100m relay in 1920 and 1924, was certain he would win the Antwerp 100m. He finished sixth and last.

" "

'If I don't do it on the first throw, I won't be able to do it at all.'

Said to a team-mate at Tokyo in 1964 by Al Oerter (USA), four times winner of the discus (1956–1968), but at Tokyo competing with an injury. In fact, it was on his *fifth* throw that he set the new Olympic record which lifted him from second to first place.

" "

'To anyone who has started out on a long campaign believing that the gold medal was destined for him, the feeling when, all of a sudden, the medal has gone somewhere else is quite indescribable.'

Britain's own Seb (later Sir Sebastian) Coe; 1500m victor at Moscow in 1980 and Los Angeles 1984; 800m runner-up in both the above games and now Chair of the London 2012 Organising Committee. The words were his reaction to losing the 800m in 1980.

" "

'I'm flabbergasted. I can't believe it. I suppose I was the only person who thought I had a chance.'

Going by the form-book, the 1964 Tokyo 10,000m should have been won by Ron Clarke (Australia), Piotr Bolotnikov (USSR) or

Murray Halberg (New Zealand). In the event, an 'unknown', the American William 'Billy' Mills, who described himself as 'seven-sixteenths Sioux Indian', won with last-gasp acceleration. Twenty years later, Mills would revisit the scene of his triumph and would run, weeping, a lonely and cathartic lap of honour.

" "

'Gosh, Herb, it looks like I won the darned thing.'

Possibly a media invention. Having pipped Jamaican's Herb McKenley at the post in the 1952 men's 100m , the American Lindy Remigino, who let this 'gosh' (or something similar) escape him.

5

DRESS

AND FASHION

'All the French girls apparently misunderstood the nature of the game scheduled for that day and turned up to play in high heels and tight skirts.'

Said by American golfer Margaret Abbott, victor at the Paris Games in 1900. Wasp-waists, long skirts and 'toothpick' leather shoes with exaggeratedly high heels were standard wear, from 1880 to 1910, for ladies engaged in golf, croquet, and even tennis and cycling; so the rationally dressed Mrs Abbott was the odd woman out. She too 'misunderstood the nature of the game'; the final was *not* (as she thought) unofficial and she was perhaps the only 'victor unawares' in Olympic history (it was only long after her dealth in 1955 that Olympic scholars found that this golf tournament was officially regarded in 1900 as an Olympic event).

" "

'The natty costumes of the Americans were a decided contrast to the home-made attire of the best European athletes who, instead of donning a sweater or bathrobe after the trials, walked about in straw hats and light overcoats.'

Unidentified journalist reporting at the Paris Games in 1900.

" "

'One of my dresses won first place in a Texas state contest in 1930.'

Mildred 'Babe' Didriksen (USA), star all-rounder of the 1932 Los Angeles Games, where she won the 80m hurdles and javelin and came second in the high jump. In the US Amateur Athletic Union (AAU) championships the same year, she set five world records in an afternoon, one of them for the baseball throw. Later, competing as Babe Zaharias, she was a tremendously popular golf champion. Her non-Olympic talents included designing and making her own golfing outfits.

" "

'The scene had a lightness and a delicacy that one has never witnessed before in England … Not a man wore his coat and many knotted their handkerchiefs round their heads…'

The Olympic correspondent of the *Manchester Guardian* looks around him in the stands of the White City during the 1948 London Games.

" "

'Their girls looked like Parisian models.'

From the *Herald Tribune* at Rome for the 1960 Olympics. Western propaganda about Soviet austerity had left the spectators and journalists quite unprepared for the entrance of the USSR delegation, on whose uniforms – the women's particularly – had been lavished the best skills of the homeland of the famous costume designers Leon Bakst and Varvara Stepanova. But the *New York Times* demonstrated a regrettable lack of chivalry by saying that 'even Yves St-Laurent could not have masked the lines of the lady shot-putters.'

" "

'The snowboarders' uniforms – hugely baggy white pants and tops with incongruous Yankee pinstripes – weren't exactly snappy; the half-pipers, who were often in a crouch, looked like moving piles of clean laundry.'

Nancy Franklin in the *New Yorker*, writing about the 2006 Turin Winter Games. In snowboarding, a 'half-pipe' is a 'U'-shaped terrain with near-vertical walls, used to perform a variety of tricks and aerial manoeuvres.

" "

'Some say the photospread is dumb, using a movie star to convey the emotions of an athlete while wearing Louboutin heels and holding $3,100 Gucci bags. I happen to disagree, I think these images are an ode to the Olympic Games and actually pay homage to the athletes who dedicate their lives to sports.'

The August 2008 issue of *Harper's Bazaar* featured a controversial photospread, entitled 'Fashion Olympics', by American photographer Peter Lindbergh, quoted above. It featured the actress Lucy Liu and was widely perceived as mocking the Olympics, and the choice of a Chinese-American model for an event held in Beijing was deplored. For the defence, the journalist pointed out that the shoot was self-evidently staged – sprinting in high heels is an impossibility. One should, he growled, look beyond the surface to the 'statement'.

" "

'Olympic figure skating – a sport where competitors are dressed as [after-] dinner mints.'

US sports writer Jeré Longman, in 2010. At the 1992 Winter Games held at Albertville in France, Maia Usova and Aleksandr Zhulin (Russia), won bronze wearing very much this costume. At the 2010 Winter Games, Russian figure-skating duo Oksana Domnina and Maxim Shabalin were widely criticised for wearing a 'variation' of Australian aboriginal sacred dress.

" "

'I will be changing the genuine fox fur in my free performance, to white faux fur.'

During Vancouver's 2010 Winter Games, skater Johnny Weir (USA) was obliged to modify his costume after protests from animal rights activists; he finished sixth.

6

ENDURANCE, OPPORTUNITY, WILL AND THE 'IMPOSSIBLE'

The Latin motto 'citius, altius, fortius', meaning 'swifter, higher, harder', is often associated with the Olympics. It was devised in 1891 by a French monk, Henri Louis Rémy Didon (1840–1900). He had been a brilliant and good-looking student, triple victor at the Wenlock-type Promenades Olympiques du Rondeau (held every four years near Grenoble between 1832 and 1906), and a young preacher admired by the Pope. His Latin motto, 'borrowed' by de Coubertin, formally entered the Olympic Games at Paris in 1924.

" "

'I haven't encountered any situation in business that even comes close to the pressure and stress you experience at the Olympics.'

Henry Marsh (USA), Los Angeles 1984, member of four Olympic teams, fourth in the 1984 men's 3000m steeplechase.

" "

'So you want to win the Olympics, pal? Chance would be a fine thing! For starters, look at the conditions and the consequences. You'll have to go into training – regular meals with no cakes, no sweets; exercise at set times whether or not you're in the mood, in hot weather or cold; no cooling drinks or wine when you feel like it. In other words, you put yourself in the hands of your coach like putting yourself in the hands of your doctor. And during the big match you'll probably dislocate your wrist, or twist your ankle, or choke on great mouthfuls of dust, or take a bashing, and eventually … lose.'

The first–second century AD Greek stoic philosopher Epictetus.

" "

'The Olympics are a lifetime of training for just ten seconds.'

Jesse – actually a teacher's misunderstanding of his initials J.C. – Owens (1913–1980), an African-American sprinter who won four gold medals (Berlin 1936). This quote was a favourite conversational remark of his and a warning to his listener that an athlete is a performer always required to give their best and that it is hazardous to get deeply involved in sport.

" "

'The Olympics is always an exercise in misery. Ten thousand people around the world start thinking it is going to be them in two years, but only one person ends up on [top of] the rostrum.'

British yachtsman Pete Newlands, who at Los Angeles in 1984 finished seventh in the mixed two-person dinghy.

" "

Georges Turlier: 'It'll do, already we've got the silver. Not bad – ease up, I can't go on…'

Jean Laudet: 'Put a sock in it, we can beat them, there's the line!'

Georges Turlier and Jean Laudet (France), Helsinki 1952 victors in the men's kayak pairs after indeed beating the Canadians to the line.

" "

Journalist: 'Why did you run barefoot?'

Abebe Bikila: 'I wanted the world to know that my country Ethiopia has always won with determination and heroism.'

At Rome 1960, the marathon victor Abebe Bikila had insisted on running barefoot over the cobblestones of the ancient Appian Way.

" "

'My country did not send me seven thousand miles away to start the race, they sent me here to finish.'

John Stephen Akhwari (Tanzania), speaking after finishing last in the 1968 marathon, which was contested in Mexico City's punishing conditions. Leaders and pack had long since finished and left, and the last few spectators were departing in the twilight, as Akhwari, leg bandaged, limping heavily, entered the stadium and, with his last ounce of strength, crossed the finishing line.

" "

'I swam my brains out.'

Mark Spitz (USA), speaking on 4 September, the day of his seventh gold medal at the Munich Olympics of 1972.

" "

Barila Bolopa: 'It was further than I thought.'

Eric Moussambani: 'I thought it was too far for me, but I made it.'

Twin 'flash quotes' from Paula Barila Bolopa and Eric Moussambani of Equatorial Guinea. Each had been entered for the Sydney 2000 Olympics through their national development programme, and had swum competitively for only a few months. Both finished last in the slowest-ever time in Olympic history (Barila Bolopa in the women's 50m and Moussambani in the men's 100m), and both to a standing ovation.

" "

'If Ian had told me before the race I would have understood. But when I saw him limping I was very angry, and said he would have to finish running.'

First in his heat in the Munich 1972 men's 5000m, Scottish runner Ian McCafferty was quietly confident of winning the final, despite running with a suspected leg muscle injury. His hopes were dashed when his leg failed him in the penultimate lap. His impulse was to drop out, but from the terraces his wife Betty, within hailing distance, ordered him to go on to the bitter end.

" "

Journalist: 'Why did you tire yourself out in the last but one lap of the race?'

Filbert Bayi: 'Because it's fun … It is fun to run as fast as you can until you are dead-tired.'

Filbert Bayi (Tanzania), speaking after finishing second in the Moscow 1980 men's 3000m steeplechase.

" "

'We started your career together, so we're going to finish this race together.'

John Redmond, father of Derek Redmond (GB), semi-finalist in the 400m in Barcelona 1992. Derek had collapsed after 150 metres with a snapped hamstring. Breaking through the cordon, his father put an arm around his son's shoulders, held his hand and led him into the home straight, letting him go on to finish unaided, to a standing ovation.

" "

'What a martyrdom! What a truly Olympic effort!'

Timoleon Philemon said this of himself. Philemon, secretary of the 1896 Organising Committee, had personally signed 2,500 official Games invitations non-stop.

" "

'Never known anything like it. All you can hear is screaming inside your head. Beethoven's Ninth, the 'Ode to Joy'… you're drowning in sound. There's something inside you that wills you to do it. Irresistible, that's how it was.'

British distance runner Chris Brasher interviewed a couple of weeks before his death in 2003, remembers his feelings when winning Olympic gold.

" "

'My will to live completely dominated my wish to win.'

Swimmer Alfréd Hajós (Guttmann-Hajós) (Hungary), 1896 victor in the 100m freestyle and 1500m (actually 1200m) freestyle. In the latter, competitors were ferried to rough open sea, where they jumped in when the starter fired his pistol. Though Hajós was smeared all over with half an inch of tallow for insulation, the icy water chilled him to the bone; he finished winner, but in severe cramp, having to be hauled out of the sea.

" "

'It seems to me one of two things will happen. Either she'll become famous all at once, or she'll give in to the pressure, do badly and lose her confidence forever.'

Xi Enting, male coach of the Chinese women's table tennis squad for Seoul 1988, pondering the career of Chen Jing, eventual winner of the women's singles. (China would go on to take all three medals in this event, at the Olympic debut of table tennis.)

" "

'Mind is everything; muscles [are nothing but] pieces of rubber. All that I am, I am because of my mind.'

Paavo Nurmi (Finland), nine times long-distance gold medallist (1920–1928) at 1500m, 5000m, 10,000m and in team cross-country. In a similar vein, the Czechoslovakian distance runner Emil Zátopek said playfully that he didn't listen to his doctor, and what happened? 'Three gold medals.'

" "

'It is horrible and yet fascinating, the struggle between a set purpose and an utterly exhausted frame. Again for a hundred yards he ran in the same furious and yet uncertain gait, and again he collapsed, kind hands saving him from a heavy fall. He was within a few yards of my seat. Amid stooping figures and grasping hands I caught a glimpse of the haggard yellow face, the glazed, expressionless eyes, the lank, black hair streaked across the brow. Surely he is done now, he cannot rise again … He staggered up, no trace of intelligence upon the set face, and again the red legs broke into their automatic amble. Will he fall again? No, he sways, he balances and he is through the tape and into a score of friendly arms. He has gone to the extreme of human endurance.'

From a ringside seat provided by the *Daily Mail* in exchange for his newspaper article, Arthur Conan Doyle, Scottish medic and creator of Sherlock Holmes, records the Italian Dorando Pietri's agonising marathon at the London 1908 Games.

" "

'You've got no hope, Clarke. You always *were* a weak bastard.'

Australian athletics coach Percy Cerutty, in his unorthodox manner, contemptuously writes off Australian runner Ron Clarke, minutes before the start of the 1964 men's 5000m at Tokyo. Often bizarre in his behaviour, Cerutty was routinely evicted from Olympic villages, and at the moment at Rome in 1960 when his protégé Herb Elliott won the 1500m, Cerutty was languishing in jail for being drunk and disorderly.

" "

'Americans never quit.'

Major-General Douglas MacArthur's response in Amsterdam to a request from the USA team to withdraw their boxing contingent from the Games, after what they thought an unfair refereeing decision. MacArthur was National Olympic Comittee President.

" "

'These are the Olympics. You die before you quit.'

US discus thrower Al Oerter's words (their authenticity debatable) when meeting his doctors during the Tokyo 1964 Games and deciding, against their advice and only a week before the event, that he was fit to compete. He won.

" "

'If you believe in yourself, you will win tomorrow.'

Film actress Mary Pickford, 'America's Sweetheart', to Charlie Paddock on the eve of the 1924 men's 200m. He was narrowly beaten at the tape.

" "

'The biggest thing in any Olympics is to have self-confidence and belief. Mary came in with her gold medal, threw it at me, and told me to go out there and get one.'

'Mary' is British long jumper Mary Rand, gold medallist at Tokyo in 1964, while speaking is Lynn Davies, eventual men's gold medallist in the same discipline that year. Her words of encouragement obviously had the desired effect.

" "

'The human body can do *so* much. Then the heart and spirit must take over.'

Sohn Kee-chung (also known as Son Kitei), South Korean but running for his country's then occupiers Japan, to reporters after his marathon victory at Berlin in 1936.

" "

'One chance is all you need.'

Jesse Owens.

" "

'I looked at the tape just forty yards away and realized that this was the only chance I would ever have to win the Olympics.'

Thomas Courtney (USA), 1956 victor in the 800m.

'At an Olympic Games you want to enjoy it, especially if you know it's going to be your last one.'

Shannon Miller (USA), winner of five gold medals at Barcelona 1992 in women's gymnastics. After his 1952 marathon victory, Zátopek confessed that: 'I was unable to walk for a whole week after that ... but it was the most pleasant exhaustion I have ever known.'

" "

'You [have] got to try and reach for the stars, or try and achieve the unreachable.'

Australian runner Cathy Freeman, 2004 in an echo of the Swedish explorer Sven Hedin's official Olympic speech in 1936 at Berlin: 'Do not be content with what you can do, strive to do the unattainable.'

" "

'At one training session I jumped so high I couldn't believe it and I didn't tell anybody. I was too frightened that if I boasted, I wouldn't be able to do it again.'

Dorothy Tyler(-Odam), British high jump silver medallist in 1936 and 1948.

" "

'In my wildest dreams I thought we could win, but not in any other frame of mind.'

British yachtsman Michael McIntyre, victor in the Seoul 1988 mixed-star class.

" "

'I don't know my own limits. Everything came to me so quickly in the final ... I finished as if I was in a dream.'

Viktor Markin (USSR), double gold medallist in 1980 (400m and 4×400m relay).

" "

(*Long jump by Bob Beamon. Shocked silence.*)

Bob Beamon: 'How far is that, Ralph?'

Ralph Boston: 'That's over 28 feet.'

Lynn Davies: 'With his first jump? No, it can't be.'

Bob Beamon: 'What do I do now? Ralph, I know you're going to kick my ass.'

Ralph Boston: 'No, no, it's over for me. I can't jump that far.'

Bob Beamon: 'What about the Great Britain dude? And what about the Russian?'

Igor Ter-Ovanesian (*to Davies*): 'We look like children.'

Lynn Davies (*to Boston*): 'I can't go on. What's the point? We'll all look silly.'

Lynn Davies (*to Beamon*): 'You have destroyed this event.'

This almost operatic exchange beside the long jump pit at Mexico City in October 1968 was between competitors Bob Beamon (USA), Ralph Boston (USA), Lynn Davies (GB) and Igor Ter-Ovanesian (USSR). Beamon later said: 'I stood there for a minute and I said, you know, I feel good. I feel like I'm going to do something special.' Then followed his monstrous long jump of 8.90m. Later, to satisfy royal curiosity, his record distance of 29 feet 2¼ inches was chalked out at Windsor Castle on the carpet of one of the endless corridors. 'Simply not possible!' was said to have been the Queen's response.

" "

Nadia Comăneci: 'What's up with the 1?'

Teammate: 'They can't do a 10.'

The great Romanian girl gymnast, winner of three individual gold medals at Montreal in 1976 (all-around, uneven bars and beam) and two at Moscow in 1980 (beam and floor). Her 1976 uneven bars routine was the first ever flawless performance in the Olympics – a '10'; it caught the Canadian organisers quite unprepared. Hastily, the scoreboard operators did the best they could: '1.00'. Puzzled by her apparently low score, Comăneci turned to her team-mate for explanation, and the truth slowly dawned.

7

FAIR PLAY,
FOUL PLAY AND DOPING

'Fair play's a jewel.'

Proverb.

" "

'Deadly enough was the strife of those chieftains heated in combat,
Yet did they part from the battle united in friendship together.'

Homer, as quoted at an official Olympic banquet in 1908 by W. Hayes Fisher, president of the English National Skating Association.

" "

'It's not like home, but I think the Olympics is about sportsmen being together.'

Edwin Moses (USA), twice gold medallist in 400m hurdles (Montreal 1976 and Atlanta 1984), in a newspaper interview.

" "

'Were strife the essential thing, would this not show in archery? But actually archers go up [to compete] bowing politely and making way for one another; and when they come down, they drink together. So even when competing, they remain perfect gentlemen.'

Confucius, *Analects* iii.7

" "

'Such are the fortunes of the game
And those who play should stop the same
By wholesome laws…
… as, long a-gone,
When men were first a nation grown,
Lawless they liv'd, till wantonness
And liberty began t' increase,
And one man lay in another's way;
Then laws were made to keep fair play.'

A century before the first modern Olympic Games, in 1896, the English visionary poet William Blake, a believer in the ethical value of sport, was already making 'fair play' a life ideal. The lines are from his 1783 poem 'Blind Man's Buff' (1783).

" "

'Though a runner in the stadium should try as hard as he can to win, he must never cut in on a fellow competitor or bump him with his arm. So also in life: it is not wrong for one to try and satisfy one's needs, but it is wrong for one to grab something from somebody else.'

The first-century BC Roman lawyer and statesman Cicero, advocating fair play at the Olympic Games, which he liked to attend.

" "

'And it's not for the sake of a ribboned coat,
Or the selfish hope of a season's fame,
But his Captain's hand on his shoulder smote –
"Play up! Play up! And play the game!"'

Sir Henry Newbolt. In this celebrated, much-mocked and much-loved quatrain from 'Vitai Lampada' (1892), 'the game' can variously be interpreted as cricket, the strategic tussle between England and Russia in Central Asia or the 'game of life'.

" "

'The Olympic Idea is to us the concept of strong muscular culture supported on one side by the spirit of chivalry – "fair play", as you so prettily call it here – and on the other by an aesthetic notion, the cultivation of all that is fine and graceful.'

Baron de Coubertin, speaking at an International Olympic Committee banquet in July 1908. Hungarian deputy and National Olympic Committee president Dr Arpád de Musza, in an official letter of thanks to the British organisers of the 1908 Games, praised their Council as 'the acme of sportsmanlike fair play'.

" "

'When De Mezo failed to understand the English language and took Starter Delany's word to "set" to mean to "go", [the American lads courteously] refused to allow him to be penalized for making a false break.'

Belo de Mezo (Hungary) was running the 100-yard dash in the 1904 Olympics at St. Louis, Missouri. He was luckier than foreign athletes at the 1906 'intercalated' Olympic Games in Athens, where in the heats of this event the start was given in modern Greek. Many runners 'were shot off the mark, and some were left,' said the US Olympic official and eyewitness James E. Sullivan.

" "

'When they knocked on the door to call us to the fight, we looked up at each other and started to cry and hugged. Ten minutes later we were beating the hell out of each other.'

American boxer Jackie Fields, 1924 featherweight gold medallist, shared a dressing-room with the opponent he would go on to defeat in the final, his compatriot Joe Salas.

" "

'Please remember, folks, that these people are our guests.'

At the Los Angeles Games in 1932, the Games' Technical Director Bill Henry appealed for calm over the PA system as home spectators booed Lauri Lehtinen (Finland), winner by just 50cm in the men's 5000m, for his blocking tactics against runner-up Ralph Hill (USA).

" "

Alain Mimoun: 'Aren't you going to congratulate me, Emil? *I* won.'

Emil Zátopek (*whips off his cap, gives Mimoun a big hug*): 'Alain, I'm so happy for you.'

The Melbourne 1956 marathon, in which Zátopek (for Czechoslovakia) finished an absent-minded sixth. Mimoun (for France), the winner, would later comment that, for him, Zátopek's congratulations were better than the medal itself.

" "

'Not for friendship's sake, but because you deserve it.'

Whispered in 1966 at Prague Airport by Emil Zátopek, to his house guest, Australian middle- and long-distance runner Ron Clarke, third in the 1964 men's 10,000m. As he saw Clarke on to the plane, Zátopek gave him a small packet, telling him to open it only when the flight was on its way and out of Czechoslovakian airspace. Clarke, suspecting that he'd been set up – as was common enough in those days – to smuggle something out to the free world, went to the aircraft lavatory and opened the packet. In it, bearing Clarke's name and the date, was the second of Zátopek's gold medals (1952) for the 10,000m. 'I sat on that toilet seat,' wrote Clarke, 'and I wept.'

" "

FAIR PLAY, FOUL PLAY AND DOPING   45

'I apologise to Yun and his mother. The gold medal is won together by them and me.'

The South Korean Judo Association had selected Kim Jae-yup as its extra-lightweight competitor at Seoul, thus causing the expected choice, Yun Hyun, loss of face, an especially serious matter in Korea. Kim made the above apology through the press, and his exemplary behaviour resulted in a substantial lifetime special government pension.

" "

'The other bloke won it fair and square, so what can you say, good luck to him. If that's the biggest disappointment in my life, then I can handle it.'

Seoul 1988 kayak singles bronze medallist Grant Davies (Australia). Light-middleweight boxer Shawn O'Sullivan (Canada), when losing after a controversial decision in the Los Angeles 1984 final for which he was favourite, likewise philosophised: 'There's no gain crying over spilt milk.'

" "

'English unfair in Olympic Games! US protests against method of holding the Tug of War. Liverpool team wears monstrous shoes that arouse ire of Americans who kick in vain.'

Ponderous *New York Times* headline during the London 1908 Games. In the finals of the tug of war the US team had come fifth and last. The silver medallists – the Liverpool Police team – wore steel-shod 'bovver boots'. They did though offer – considerately or ironically? – to compete in their socks. But the Americans said nope.

" "

'"Any competitor who cheated or took bribes could be publicly flogged," I said, as we gazed at the dreary length of the stadium.

"What a pity," said Alexis, "that this regulation has been discarded from the modern Olympics."'

The racy novelist, gentleman gambler and unfrocked classicist Simon Raven, in his memoir *Is there anybody there? said the traveller* (1990). The narrator is visiting ancient Olympia with boyfriend Alexis.

'It is very doubtful whether it was quite within the spirit of the Olympic ideal of true sportsmanship to field players who are – week in, week out – assisting England's leading professional [soccer] teams to win their matches.'

A gentle reproof in the 1913 Stockholm Official Report. It was an iron rule of the International Olympic Committee that no one who made any kind of living from sport (with the sole exception of the 'chivalrous' fencing-master) should be allowed to compete in the Games. British professional soccer had started with Blackburn Olympic's cup final in 1883.

" "

'I could not speak for tears. I threw the silver medal out of the window ... Always I had respected the cleanness and impartialness of contests of strength. That night I knew there is one kind of strength in which there is no justice.'

Yuri Petrovich Vlasov (USSR). In September 1960, Soviet newspaper *Pravda* had pictured the 'endless applause' as the crowd raised Ukrainian super-heavyweight weightlifter and poet Vlasov, the 'Strongest Man on the Planet', shoulder-high after his victory. In 1964 he won only the silver medal mentioned above, not the expected gold, and retired disillusioned. Why? Because in the first stages of the final, his fellow Ukrainian and weightlifter Leonid Ivanovich Zhabotinski had come up to the trusting Vlasov and pretended to sportingly concede defeat. Then, with his last attempt, Zhabotinski exerted himself and won (as he would also in 1968) the gold medal.

" "

'I did not attack the right side [of Yamashita] because this is against my principles. I would not want to win this way.'

Principles? At Los Angeles in 1984, the Japanese men's judo athlete Yasuhiro Yamashita, eventual open victor, competed with an injured right leg against Mohamed Ali Rashwan of Egypt, who was presumably party to the traditional Olympic Oath (to play fair) sworn by one athlete on behalf of all at the Opening Ceremony. Though the International Committee awarded Rashwan its Trophy for Fair Play on the strength of his words, the video recording showed that he had in fact instantly attacked Yamashita's right leg. But the Trophy was never withdrawn and Rashwan remains the official silver medallist.

" "

'What you fellows need to warm up is a glass of sherry and a raw egg.'

After his own Olympic achievements – fifth in the 100-yard dash at St. Louis in 1904, and gold and silver in long jump and high jump respectively, at the Athens Games of 1906 – Lawson Robertson coached the USA team from 1912 to 1936, his training methods showing the influence of his Scottish roots. The recipe quoted helped Charlie Paddock (USA) win the 100m in 1920.

" "

'Before the race his trainer had given him a shot of opium to provide additional stamina.'

America's George Patton, the future general, ahead of his pentathlon final at Stockholm in 1912, where he finished fifth behind four Swedes. The 'hop' probably did him little good, comments his biographer.

" "

'Who wants some piss?'

Britain's 1968 boxing middleweight gold medallist Chris Finnegan had problems when waiting for his urine test. Only after consuming multiple glasses of water, four pints of beer and a victory meal, was he able, in the wee hours, to finally provide, along with the above quote, a 'specimen'.

" "

'It shouldn't have surprised anyone that Ben Johnson was using steroids. You don't go from 10.17 to 9.83 [seconds] on unleaded gas.'

Jamaican-born Ben Johnson ran for Canada at Seoul 1988, winning the 100m. As his doping test revealed steroid use, the IOC Medical Commission recommended he be disqualified, and two days later Johnson was stripped of his gold medal, despite his claim that 'I have never knowingly taken illegal drugs'. The comment above is from Johnson's doctor and supplier Jamie Astaphan.

'We have made drugs an Olympic event.'

US decathlete and Olympic victor at Mexico City 1968, Bill Toomey, pointing out that the issue of doping receives a great deal of coverage at the Games and even suspected use of banned substances can ruin an athlete's reputation for life.

" "

'I'm sure Chinese sport is very clean.'

Seventh International Olympic Committee president Juan Antonio Samaranch, blasé, despite the suspension of eleven Chinese athletes for testing positive before or at the 1994 Asian Games.

8
FAME
AND OBLIVION

'Number one, obviously, the fame, it brings people to the party.'

Carl Lewis, the 100m specialist and nine times Olympic gold medallist, in an interview in 2010. Here 'the party' is the fight against world hunger that Lewis is involved with through his charity work.

" "

'So I want to make this piece called the "Olympic Militia" project. I want to explore the concept that competitive sport, at its highest level, also serves as the highest expression of the pursuit of glory.'

Gabe Jennings (USA), middle-distance runner, successful Olympic trialist, didgeridoo-player and self-proclaimed 'man of extremes', talking to *Runners' World* about his art piece project.

" "

'I told them "I did more for your country than all your textiles, all your exports".'

Vitaly Scherbo (USSR and Belarus), is considered by many to be the greatest of all Olympic male gymnasts. His bravura, accuracy and sense of occasion secured him six gold medals at Barcelona in 1992. Here he flays his national officials…

" "

'I would rather have won this race than be president of the United States.'

English-born American Thomas Hicks, speaking after his 1904 marathon victory.

" "

'My time has passed, but you can't take away what I did.'

The great American sprinter and long-jumper Carl Lewis, nine times Olympic victor, speaking at the end of his career.

" "

'If you win, you're lasting.'

The 'Flying Finn', Lasse Virén, long-distance specialist and double Olympic victor (5000m, 10,000m) at Munich in 1972 and again at Montreal in 1976.

" "

'I heard people calling my name – and I couldn't realise how one fellow could have so many friends.'

Jim Thorpe (USA), won the pentathlon and decathlon at the 1912 Stockholm Games with ease and on successive days. New York welcomed him home with a huge ticker-tape reception. But at the start of 1913 a press-hound discovered that Thorpe had received $25 a week to play baseball. He begged for this to be overlooked, but the American Amateur Athletic Union disowned him and the International Olympic Committee stripped him of his medals.

" "

'If he [Michael Phelps] wins seven golds and ties what I did, then it would be like I was the first man on the Moon and he became the second. If he wins more than seven, then he becomes the first man on Mars.'

Swimmer Mark Spitz (USA) at Munich 1972 won seven gold medals (four individual: 100m and 200m in both freestyle and butterfly; and three team relay). His fellow American Phelps went on to indeed become the 'first man on Mars', after winning eight golds and setting seven world records in the process.

66 99

'Olympic gold changed me and my life dramatically. I became a celebrity overnight and people see me as a famous skater, not a real person.'

Oksana Baiul (Ukraine), women's figure skating gold medallist at Lillehammer Winter Olympics in 1994.

66 99

'Nobody looks askance at the praise bestowed on an Olympic victor.'

Pindar (c. 552–443 BC), Greek composer of cantatas to flatter Olympic victors – in this case the winner of the boys' boxing, a lad from Greek southern Italy, in the year 476 (*Olympian Cantata*, xi.7–8).

66 99

'I saw the torments of Salmoneus in Hell, for aping the earsplitting thunder of Olympian Zeus, Salmoneus who drove his chariot on a victory parade through Greece, brandishing a torch, and even through Olympia itself, demanding to be honoured like a god – the fool!'

The first-century Roman poet Vergil is observing the souls of the damned and reflecting on the foolish pride of some victorious athletes – as relevant today as it was then.

66 99

'Since he became an Olympic champion, Armin Hary has been acting up like Maria Callas.'

Unidentified French journalist in *Le Miroir des Sports*. Hary (West Germany) had won the men's 100m and 4×100m at the 1960 Rome Games. Callas was a great and temperamental Greek-Italian opera singer, renowned for her occasional diva-like behaviour.

" "

'I had always imagined an Olympic champion was something more than a mere mortal, in fact, a god. Now I knew he was just a human being.'

Sir Murray Gordon Halberg (NZ), 1960 victor in the men's 1500m. Dan O'Brien (USA), 1996 decathlon victor echoed the sentiment: 'It took me time to realise that the men who win Olympic gold medals in the decathlon are just men, like me.'

" "

'All I did was win some foot races.'

Fanny Blankers-Koen (Netherlands), while watching the huge parade in her honour in Amsterdam. She had returned from the 1948 London Games as its acknowledged star, with four gold medals: one team (4×100m relay) and three individual (100m, 200m and 85m hurdles).

" "

'I'm just a girl who runs.'

Blurted out by shy South African Zola Budd (competing for Great Britain to circumvent the boycott of South African athletes during apartheid) to journalists, after being unwillingly involved in a notorious collision in the 3000m in Los Angeles 1984 (where she finished seventh).

" "

'I only did what anyone would have done. We all like to win. After all, I'm only an Olympic victor by nine centimetres.'

Noemí Simonetto de Portela (Argentina) speaking after winning the London 1948 women's long jump.

'Won. George.'

Canadian George Goulding's minimalist telegram to his wife after winning the 10,000m walk at Stockholm 1912. The silver medal for economy of phrasing goes to French small-bore rifle marksman Pierre Coquelin de Lisle who telegraphed to his mother in 1924: 'Suis champion Olympique. Record mondial battu. Arrriverai mardi matin.' ('Am Olympic champion. World Record beaten. Arriving Tuesday morning.')

" "

(*Before*): 'Only frivolous people practise sport instead of studying.'

(*After*): 'Your medals leave me cold, I am just anxious to hear how you perform in your next examination.'

Lajos Ilosvay, Dean of Faculty at Budapest Polytechnic University, to Alfred Hajós in 1896 before Hajós went to the first modern Olympic Games and came back double victor in swimming. Despite his stiff academic attitude, Ilosvay was actually pro-sport. Hajós passed with distinction and Ilosvay did the decent thing and congratulated him.

" "

'Finishing second in the Olympics gets you silver. Finishing second in politics gets you oblivion.'

Richard Nixon, the former US President, speaking in 1988.

" "

'I am forgotten. No one remembers who I was ... Sometimes I think, "Oh, dear, oh, dear, how good I must have been, how really *good*"!'

As a 17-year-old, Netherlands swimmer 'Rie' Mastenbroek (1919– 2003) had won three gold medals at Berlin in 1936 – two individual (women's freestyle 100m and 400m) and one team (4×100m freestyle relay) – plus silver in the 100m backstroke.

" "

'When I got home after London I thought people would soon forget – but I don't think they are going to, are they?'

Fanny Blankers-Koen, interviewed fifty years after her triumphs of 1948.

" "

'I want to do wild things at this Olympics – that's my focus. I want, at the end of the Games, for people to sit down and say, "Did that really happen?"'

Usain Bolt (Jamaica), the new world record holder for the men's 100m, with his astonishing and carefree victory at the 2012 Beijing Games; he also took gold in the 200m and the 4×100m relay. This wish of his for the 2012 London Games make the Olympics, both for athletes and spectators, an interface between actuality and dream, between history and myth.

9
FINE ART
AND BEAUTY

For Carl Diem, secretary of the 1936 Organising Committee, the Olympics were no array of competitions or test of human limits, but rather a study in aesthetics.

" "

'A race is a work of art that people can look at and be affected by in as many ways as they're capable of understanding.'

Distance-runner Steve Prefontaine (USA), who finished fourth in the 5000m at Munich in 1972.

" "

'I wanted Rome because only there, on its return from its trip to utilitarian America, could Olympism reclothe itself in the sumptuous toga, woven of art and thought, in which I had wanted to reclothe it.'

Baron de Coubertin, is angling, in his usual wordy way, to have Rome, not London, as the host city after the 1906 Athens Games.

'Some people wonder why fine arts should be in the Olympics. Why shouldn't they be? The Greeks had them. And sport itself is a fine art. Yes, a fine art.'

Avery Brundage, fifth president of the International Olympic Committee, in an interview in 1952, riding a hobbyhorse of his.

❝ ❞

'He broke with custom by having a "music and culture" event included in the Olympic Games.'

The Roman emperor Nero, as reported by the historian Suetonius, toys with the make-up of the Games. International Olympic Committee president Juan Antonio Samaranch defined Olympism as 'the marriage of sport and culture'.

❝ ❞

'Here shall be an open air temple of Swedish granite sculpture, the very finest that we can produce. Severe and warlike rises the remainder of the northern Stadium. But in this little park, the sunshine playing through the crowns of oaks in mystic clare-obscure, a vision shall be given of *Man* – of strength and beauty, carried monumentally on the pilaster-strips of the sturdy walls.'

Swedish architect Torbén Grut imagines the South Arcade of the 1912 Stockholm Olympic Complex. 'Clare-obscure' means 'light and shade'.

❝ ❞

'Shoot more of him! Shoot more of him! Everywhere shoot more of him, he is beautiful!'

Leni Riefenstahl, German director of the breathtaking film *Olympia*, a poetic record of the Berlin 1936 Olympics, sees only beauty in the physical movement of compatriot and athlete Heinz Von Jaworski.

❝ ❞

'Sport changed from being a jumbled striving of individual athletes and teams to a new unity, with a beauty that is evident in man's highest endeavour. The debt of loyalty that I had reserved for Oxford I now found I owed to a whole world.'

Watching the 1948 Olympic Games at the age of 19 completely altered the attitude of Roger Bannister, fourth in the 1500m in his only Olympics (Helsinki 1952) but 21 months later the first four-minute miler, to the sport that he was by now heavily involved in.

" "

'[Her] floor exercises ... so beautifully exemplified youth, beauty and joy that when she had finished, we simply stood up and cried.'

Veteran *Times* tennis correspondent Rex Bellamy remembers Ukrainian Soviet gymnast Larisa Latynina, the only female athlete to win nine Olympic gold medals (at Rome in 1960 and Tokyo in 1964).

" "

'In the dance you can simultaneously find film, comics, the Olympic 100 metres, swimming, plus poetry, love, and tenderness as well. That's what the twentieth century is.'

The French choreographer Maurice Béjart, in his autobiography *Un Instant dans la Vie*. In 1968, Béjart had choreographed a piece for the Grenoble Winter Games festival.

" "

'Art makes the Olympics more beautiful.'

Mindful of the Chinese tradition of calligraphy, the Organising Committee for the Games of the XXIX Olympiad decided that art competitions must be included in the Olympics for Beijing 2008, for the first time since the 1950s, but this time with prizes, not medals. The requirement was a sport-related work in architecture, literature, music, painting or sculpture. The competition was advertised with the above slogan, which looks even better in Chinese.

10
FOOD, DRINK AND PARTYING

Two elements which bulk large in big sporting events, and especially the Olympic Games, are athletes' diets and spectators' consumption of (sponsored) food and drink. Sometimes, as at the Paralympic Games in Athens, the organisers seem almost to be boasting about the amount of planetary resources they have demolished.

" "

'Pythagoras took it on himself to train a competitor named Eurymenes from his own island of Samos. Thanks to Pythagoras's wise words, and despite being small in build, Eurysthenes defeated many a heftier opponent at Olympia. Whereas his competitors stuck to the traditional diet of cheese and figs, he followed his trainer's advice and ate a set daily quota of meat – the first athlete ever to do so – thus making his body stronger.'

A biographical detail, possibly pure invention, about the famous sixth-century BC mathematician, in Porphyrios's treatise 'Abstaining from Animal Meat', written in AD 270 or thereabouts.

'On one occasion [Carvajal] stopped at [my] automobile, where a party were eating peaches, and begged for some. Being refused, he playfully snatched two, and ran along the road, eating them as he ran.'

At 29, Félix Carvajal de Soto (Cuba) was the oldest participant in the St. Louis 1904 marathon. The author, C. J. P. Lucas (USA), was head official and monitoring the marathon from his car.

" "

'Exposure to the unlimited menus onboard was fatal to some and several hopes of Olympic victory foundered at the bounteous dinner table.'

At age 24, US athlete Avery Brundage sailed from New York to Stockholm to compete in the pentathlon (fifth) and decathlon (did not finish), in the 1912 Games.

" "

'This disgusting event marked the only time in Olympic history when animals were killed on purpose.'

The Paris 1900 live pigeon shooting event, here commented on with distaste in the Official Report, was held at club premises in the Bois de Boulogne and attracted record numbers. The hamburgers eaten by spectators in 2012 will, of course, have been killed by accident.

" "

'I went looking for our food and there was a lovely smell coming from the house next door and I joined the queue. I think it must have been the French team. That's the sort of spirit in which one went off to the Games.'

Mary Alina Glen Haig, the young British fencer who finished eighth in foil at the 1948 London Games, was here making an enterprising forage in the Olympic Village.

" "

'French athletes attribute some of their failures at the Games to insufficient food.'

London 1948 again and Reuters reported strong complaints from visiting athletes billeted in private houses in Wembley about the lack of meal facilities.

" "

'There was a brass band of many pieces. There was champagne – much of it – and, until we were able to explain the reason for our abstinence, international complications threatened. Training? A strange word. Come, a glass of wine to pledge friendship. No? Strange people, these Americans.'

Athenian hospitality came up against the American training system in 1896, in this account by lawyer Ellery Harding Clark (USA), who won gold in the high jump and long jump.

" "

'Refreshments en route – The Oxo Company have been appointed Official Caterers and will supply the following free of charge to competitors: Oxo Athletes' Flask, containing Oxo for immediate use. Oxo hot and cold; Oxo and soda, rice pudding, raisins, bananas, soda and milk. Stimulants will be available in cases of collapse.'

Instructions to marathon competitors, London 1908.

" "

'A gold medallist shouldn't be drinking chocolate.'

An Australian weightlifter takes exception to American diving victor Maxine King's choice of beverage at Munich 1972.

" "

'I was on the piss last night, sorry mate.'

Bevan Docherty of New Zealand, in response to journalist Nick Willis in 2008. Docherty was a non-starter in the Beijing 2008 men's 1500m, and gives a disarmingly honest explanation at the press conference of how he came to miss his race.

'What was really lovely about the '48 Olympics was that we had a marvellous rowing party afterwards, and it was the most splendid get-together I've ever been to and I feel now it's much more technically superior, of course, but on the other hand I think it's lost a lot of the amateur spirit.'

Oarsman Robert Collins (GB) competed in the London 1948 men's coxed fours; the British crew was eliminated in the heats by the eventual winners, the USA.

" "

'At the Olympics, I always felt the partying could wait because I'd rather go home with a medal.'

Shannon Miller (USA), winner of five gold medals in women's gymnastics at Barcelona in 1992.

" "

'Me, it's been an awesome two weeks. I got to party and socialize at an Olympic level.'

Alpine skier Bode Miller (USA), super combined victor at Vancouver 2010. The quotation is from an interview in 2006 with Associated Press which brought down the wrath of sponsors, fans and media about Miller's ears.

" "

'It was bloody awful food, and after a while the Americans started throwing the bread rolls around, saying they weren't fit to eat. So we all started pelting each other with the food. In the end somebody shoved a custard tart down some bloke's neck and he turned round and sloshed him, so I left before it got any nastier – which it did.'

Sculler, Bert Bushnell (Great Britain), London 1948 gold medallist, remembering the *start* of the 1948 celebration dinner for all Olympic rowers.

11
DISCIPLINES –
GENERAL AND INDIVIDUAL

In reply to his own question, 'Why did I restore the Olympic Games?', Baron de Coubertin said 'To ennoble and strengthen sport ... For the glorification of the individual athlete, whose muscular activity is necessary for the maintenance of the general spirit of competition.'

" "

'The Games were as bewildering to watch as a three-ring circus. At one time a dozen bicyclists were wheeling along the outer edges of the oval, while twenty runners were racing on the cinder path just inside of it.'

New York Times correspondent commenting on numerous disciplines being contested at once (now standard practice) in the White City arena at London 1908.

Track and field

'We come here, as we went to Paris and Athens, with a field team, and are making a fight in the field events, caring little for the other [events].'

The USA's 'athletics mission' to London 1908, as outlined by James E. Sullivan (USA), St. Louis 1904 Games Director.

" "

'You may win this time, but we will beat you in 1900 – *even if I have to run myself*!'

King George of the Hellenes to Thomas Burke (USA), victor in the 100m, at Athens in 1896.

" "

'Keep calm, it's only another Sunday school race.'

Canadian coach Bob Granger to Percy Williams, just before the final of the 100m at Amsterdam in 1928, which Williams unexpectedly won.

" "

'I have the killer instinct. It's ego. When I'm on the track, I want to beat everyone. An individual sport is basically a gladiator sport.'

Edwin Moses (USA), double gold medallist in 400m hurdles (1976 and 1984).

" "

'Race walking is arguably the most unnatural act that remains legal. To see a male Olympic walker in full cry is to be reminded of Barbara Windsor in a *Carry On* film, wiggling down the road in a tight skirt...'

In Geoff Tibball's *Mammoth Book of Comic Quotes* (2004).

" "

Journalist: 'Why does your nation produce so many great runners?'

Lagat: 'It's the road signs – "Beware of lions!"'

Bernard Kip Lagat (USA, formerly Kenya), runner-up in the 1500m at Athens in 2004.

" "

'The marathon contest won't be for a long time yet, so I must simply find something to do till then.'

Emil Zátopek (Czechoslovakia), teasing reporters about his impromptu entry for the 5000m at Helsinki in 1952.

Marathon

'…the subsequent epidemic of "Marathon Races" which attacked the civilized world from Madison Square Gardens to the Valley of the Nile…'

British Olympic historian Sir Theordore Cook, in 1908, comments with aristocratic disdain on the extraordinary rise of the marathon. Its popularity dated not from 1896, as might have been expected from Spyros Louis's marathon victory at Athens, but from 1908. It was on 24 July of that year that, in the memorable and much-reported climax of the Olympic marathon at London's White City, Dorando Pietri (Italy) entered the Stadium visibly at his last gasp, exciting spectators to a mixture of pity and horror.

" "

'We are different, in essence, from other men. If you want to win something, run 100 metres. If you want to experience something, run a marathon.'

Distance runner Emil Zátopek (Czechoslovakia), victor in the marathon (1952) and 10,000m (1948, 1952); runner-up (1948) and victor (1952) in the 5000m.

" "

'There is the truth about the marathon and very few of you have written the truth. Even if I explain to you, you'll never understand it.'

Douglas Wakiihuri (Kenya), runner-up in the Seoul 1988 marathon, speaking to sports journalists.

" "

'The British Ambassador immediately detailed his butler for the job and provided him with a bicycle for the purpose. The butler, though unwilling to perform this unorthodox chore, was eventually persuaded to accompany Flack – and, complete with bowler hat, pedalled in solemn attendance with the Australian favourite…'

Edwin Flack, an Australian of English origin, was thus assured of refreshments as he ran the 1896 marathon. At the 37th kilometre he collapsed and went into a hallucination, punching Greek spectators who tried to assist him. He was removed unconscious by carriage and given first aid by the Greek Prince Nicholas in person. Fortunately he recovered and lived to be 61, though he never competed again in the Olympics.

" "

'[Len Tau] lost a great deal of valuable time when he was chased off the course and through a cornfield by two large dogs. He still managed to finish ninth.'

From David Wallechinsky's *The Complete Book of the Olympics* (Aurum, 1996). The South African warrior Len Tau (meaning 'lion') Nyane had fought the British in the Boer War. Entered for the St Louis Marathon, perhaps as a curiosity, he proved to be the first of the great African marathon runners of the modern era, finishing ninth. The tale about the dogs (or dog) may or may not be founded in fact, but is too good to just ignore.

" "

'The roads were so lined with vehicles that the runners had to constantly dodge the horses and wagons. So dense were the dust clouds on the road that frequently the runners could not be seen by the automobiles following them.'

An unidentified eye-witness of the marathon race at the St Louis Games 1904.

" "

'Don't overtax your strength, darling.'

Czech javelin gold medallist Dana Zátopková gave this advice to her even more famous Czech husband, Emil Zátopek, in 1952 as he considered entering at the last minute for the 5000m. He had also been warned by his doctors not to compete because of glandular fever. Zátopek is said to have commented, tongue-in-cheek, to reporters: 'The score in the family contest is too close, I must try for the marathon'.

" "

'I was OK until the 32nd kilometre. Twelve kilometres from the finish I had a terrible wallop, it felt as if there was a house on my head. I was doing 7-inch strides. It's a terrible feeling fighting against yourself. At that moment I thought I only had one more kilometre to get through before I was Olympic champion. I was dreaming.'

French-Algerian runner Alain Mimoun's own experience of the 1956 marathon, which he won.

" "

'It was a fun 42 kilometres.'

Naoko Takahashi (Japan), women's marathon victor in Sydney 2000. Said Aouita (Morocco), after winning the Los Angeles 1984 men's 5000m, likewise told journalists 'It was a very easy run. Usually I like more of a challenge.'

Aquatic

'Jesu Christo! I'm freezing!'

American swimmer Gardner Williams, who finished unplaced in the Athens 1896 men's freestyle 100m and 1200m.

" "

'The water wasn't water – it was spaghetti … The strands tangled and tied my feet.'

Australian swimmer Dawn Fraser, 100m freestyle gold medallist (1956, 1960 and 1964), describes an anxiety dream the night before her 1956 final.

" "

'They were lucky to get out of the stadium alive.'

Swimmer Wally Wolf (USA) on the Soviet team's ignominious exit after the Melbourne 1956 water polo semi-final, the 'Blood in the Water' match. They lost it 4-0 to Hungary, the country that the USSR had invaded a few days previously.

" "

'The Olympics wasn't really considered to be so important in the sailing world. They didn't cancel Cowes Week, even though it coincided with the Games.'

Yachtsman David Bond (GB), the Torbay 1948 gold medallist in the Swallow class.

" "

Allen Warren: 'She went lame on us, so we decided the poor old 'orse should be cremated.'

David Hunt: 'My skipper has style – but not that much. I tried to persuade him to burn with the ship but he wouldn't agree.'

British yachtsmen Allen Warren and David Hunt, tempest-class runners-up in 1972 and unplaced in 1976. To fathom the above dialogue, weird enough to have come out of a play by Tom Stoppard or Samuel Beckett, you need to know the (ironic) name of Warren and Hunt's boat: *Gift 'Orse*. Blaming their 'lame' boat for their poor performance in 1976, as compared with 1972, they publicly set it on fire, in a Norse manner, after the final race.

Equestrian

'Some people get their kicks out of picking up dust in a chariot race on an Olympic track, as they hot-rod an inch from the kerb, to win the world-famous branch of palm that hoists them up, Lords of All Lands, to the gods.'

The Roman poet Horace in the very first of his *Odes* (i.1.3-4).

" "

'At the Olympics I love watching almost anything at all that's special, so long as it doesn't have a horse in it.'

British decathlete Daley Thompson.

Various

'Gentlemen will not be allowed to smoke at the Ladies' [archery] targets.'

London 1908 Regulations.

" "

'Coming after the war, the Olympics was like something out of the blue … There was a large attendance at the cycling track and the atmosphere was very exciting.'

Robert Geldard (GB), 4000m team pursuit bronze medallist at London 1948. At the time, British cycling, nowadays very big business, had started to pull the crowds. No longer could one think of it, as the British competitor in discus at the Athens 1896 Games George Robertson had done, as 'a kind of exercise, by many scarcely admitted to the domain of sport'.

" "

'The decathlon is nine Mickey Mouse events and the 1500 metres.'

Steve Ovett (GB), at Moscow in 1980 the winner of the 800m and runner-up in the 1500m.

" "

'Cornwall had weight in the scrummages but were usually beaten for the ball, especially in the open play preferred by the Australians.'

The 1908 Official Report, in the section on rugby.

" "

'Was not the French [rugby] football team's captain, two hours before the match, smoking a fat cigar with a paper band round it, whereas the whole German team had been laying off tobacco for a fortnight?'

The French journal *Tous les Sports*, reporting on the France vs Germany rugby match at the Vincennes velodrome on 14 October 1900 as part of the Paris Games. Virtue was not rewarded; 5-14 down at half time, France eventually won 27-17.

" "

'South American [association] football held the place of honour, thanks to Uruguay's victory, and it was indeed the best team that won … They tired their opponents with short passes, thus gaining ground…'

In the 1924 Paris Games, Uruguay, having defeated France by five goals to one, convincingly won their final against Switzerland.

" "

'Ping pong is coming home.'

Boris Johnson, Mayor of London, getting it wrong at Beijing in 2008; the roots of competitive international table tennis are unquestionably Hungarian-Jewish.

" "

'This little accident seemed to put Setterwall off his game.'

At the Stockholm Games in 1912, Swedish tennis player Sigrid Fick had – accidentally – hit her mixed doubles partner Gunnar Setterwall hard in the face with her racquet. This homely detail was solemnly noted in the official report. The pair finished only second.

" "

'And I have seene thee pause and take thy breath
When that a ring of Greekes have hem'd thee in
Like an Olympian wrestling.'

William Shakespeare's *Troilus and Cressida* (1602), iv.5. How did he know about the Olympic Games and that they included wrestling? Probably from Sir Thomas North's translation (1579) of Plutarch's *Life of Theseus*, needed for his *Midsummer Night's Dream.*

" "

'It was a fight of the Police Department of Montreal against that of Greater New York.'

The final of the 56lb weight throw (no longer an Olympic event) at St Louis 1904, as recalled by American official C. J. P. Lucas in the following year. The Montreal policeman Étienne Desmarteau, with his first throw, set a target (34 feet 4 inches) that was too much for his opponent the New York policeman John Flanagan. Desmarteau died of typhoid in 1905.

" "

'It is impossible for any patriotic Englishman to take the Olympic Games seriously, for the simple reason that they exclude cricket.'

British humorist William Davis, writing in *Punch* in 1976. This had not always been so; cricket, billed as 'English throwing', under M.C.C. Rules, appeared on the provisional 1895 (though not the final 1896) programme of the first modern Olympic Games.

Winter Olympics

'The Winter Olympics is no more than forty kinds of sliding.'

Dara Ó Briain, Irish stand-up comedian.

" "

'I remember when I did my first jump, I looked from the top and I was so frightened that my bum shrivelled up like a prune.'

Skier Eddie Edwards (GB), the heroic underachiever of the Seoul 1988 Games, talking about his early days, on a film clip from about 1980.

Wishful thinking

'There is no doubt but that an Olympic mountaineering prize would lead to the loss of many human lives.'

Erik Ullén (Sweden), of the Olympic Committee for Mountain Ascents in 1912.

" "

'But then we Americans did not "include in" the athletic events, which decided the championship, such manly sports as archery, croquet, hop scotch, jack-straws, mumblety-peg, diablo and ring toss. In this kind of event the British athletes really do excel.'

An American columnist, with elephantine sarcasm, reporting on the 1908 London Games.

" "

'Ninety-seven per cent of all youth play video games, dwarfing the number of kids who participate in activities like basketball, track, and javelin throwing; that's why I'm an advocate of ruling video games an Olympic sport.'

The popular New York astrologer Bob Brezsny tries to modernise the Games.

" "

American: 'I'm rooting for the USA.'

Australian: 'Strewth – it's an Olympic event?'

12
MEDALS

The original prize for victory at the Olympic Games was just a branch of wild olive made into a crown and placed on the winner's head. There was no medal, no money, no raising of the flag. Nor did the ancient Greeks keep, and nor could they have done, precise time-and-space measurements of performance. Consequently, by contrast with today, records did not matter.

" "

Iranian scout: 'The Greeks are holding their Olympic Games.'

Tritantachmes: 'What is the prize?'

Iranian scout: 'A garland of olive leaves.'

Tritantachmes: 'Great God Almighty! What kind of people have you brought us here to fight? What they are competing against each other for is not a material prize but – honour!'

In 480 BC, an Iranian officer in Xerxes's invasion army, expecting to add Greece to the Persian Empire, discovers from a spy that the enemy's values are superior to his own. A story from Herodotus's *Histories*.

'I have "run a good race", "finished the course", and "kept faith" [i.e. observed the Athletes' Oath]. So a wreath, and a well-merited one, is waiting for me and will be awarded to me by the Lord on the day of judging; for me, and to all who have done him credit. So put on speed and come to me quickly.'

Paul of Tarsus, 2 Timothy 4:7–8.

" "

'The Olympic wreath is, as you know, only olive branches, but many have honoured it more than life itself.'

Dio Chrysostom, writing in around AD 100. The motto of ancient Greek athletes at Olympia was 'The wreath – or death!'

" "

'And if we thrive, promise them such rewards

As Victors were at the Olympian Games.'

William Shakespeare's *Henry VI, Part III* (1591) ii.3.

" "

'The names having been read, the winning athletes were summoned to a carpeted platform in front of the Royal Box to receive their prizes. In a loud voice, the Herald announced the victor's name, country, and event. The athlete then received his certificate and medal from the King. For the winner there was a silver medal [with the head of Zeus and a relief of the Parthenon] and a branch of wild olive; for the runner-up a bronze medal and a branch of laurel.'

The awards to winners at Athens at the first modern Olympics in 1896, here described by historian Konstantinos Georgiadis. How very different from nowadays! The certificate was protected by a cardboard cylinder tastefully trimmed with gold paper.

The tidy modern award system – gold to the winner of an Olympic event, silver to the runner-up and bronze to the third-placed – was introduced only in 1904. Thus Spyros Louis, the archetypal marathon winner in 1896, was not a 'gold medallist' but a 'victor'. Arrangements could be rather casual in the early days: Harold

Abrahams received his medals – gold for 100m individual, silver for 4×100m team relay – by surface mail one month after the Paris 1924 Games; and as the French authorities had carelessly understamped the package, he had to pay the excess postage himself.

" "

'Each [medal] was tied with a small silken Union Jack, and the precedent so gracefully set with the olive leaves presented by the King of Greece in Athens was thus carried out in our own country with the appropriate symbol of the national oak.'

London 1908. The symbolic oak leaves came from Windsor Forest, as the prizegiving programme proudly proclaims.

" "

'Our high reputation for sportsmanlike behaviour is of course vastly more important to us than any number of gold and silver medals.'

The Times, July 1908 (this was not, however, the opinion of the American press). Mary Alina Glen Haig, British fencing veteran of the Olympics from 1948 to 1960, confirmed during an interview in 2008 that 'Things like winning medals, we didn't worry about things like that in those days'.

" "

'If you don't try to win you might as well hold the Olympics in somebody's back yard. The thrill of competing carries with it the thrill of a gold medal. One wants to win to prove himself the best.'

The American sprint maestro of the 1936 Berlin Olympics, Jesse Owens, in his 1978 autobiography (written with Paul Neimark).

" "

'I see my career as a château. My silver medal at London is the foundation, my two silvers at Helsinki are the walls, and the gold at Melbourne put the roof on.'

French distance runner Alain Mimoun, second to Zátopek in the 10,000m at London in 1948 and again at Helsinki in 1952. He was at last to win his gold in the Melbourne 1956 marathon. Joan Benoit Samuelson, 1984 women's marathon gold medallist, imagined her victories differently, as 'milestones on a very long highway'.

" "

'An Olympic medal is the greatest achievement and honour that can be received by an athlete. I would swap my world title to have a gold at the Olympics.'

Boxer Jeff Fenech (Australia), fifth at Los Angeles in 1984 at flyweight, and thrice world champion.

" "

'Every record set in Montreal will eventually be broken and forgotten. The gold medal is the thing they can't take away from you.'

John Walker (New Zealand), 1976 victor in the 1500m.

" "

'What does it matter if they are with me or somewhere else?'

Finnish distance runner Lasse Virén, in October 1994, talking teasingly about selling off his four gold medals (for the 5000m and the 10,000m both at Munich 1972 and Montreal 1976). He put a value of US$200,000 on each.

" "

'I wouldn't say that there's ever been an Olympic champion that didn't deserve to win an Olympic gold medal.'

Figure skater Dorothy Hamill (USA), Montreal 1976 gold medallist.

" "

'I've got the Big G, boys – the Big G!'

Daley Thompson (GB), twice decathlon victor in 1980 and 1984. Daley was regarded as highly 'quotable', and he relished controversy, for instance his description of a rival caught doping as 'a cheating bastard who should be banned from the [Olympic] Games for life'.

" "

'It's good for the ego being a small part of a large picture. If I came away with a medal, it would be the highlight of my year. If I came away with a gold, it would be the highlight of my life.'

Pam Shriver (USA), women's tennis doubles victor (with Zina Garrison) at Seoul 1988.

" "

'My goal is one Olympic gold medal. Not many people in this world can say, "I'm an Olympic gold medallist".'

Swimmer Michael Phelps (USA), a specialist in medley and butterfly, speaking before his record haul of eight golds in Beijing in 2008.

" "

'Give them *both* the gold medal!'

Italian fans in the 1960 Rome decathlon; it was uncertain up to the last minutes of the last event (the 1500m) whether Rafer Johnson (USA) or Yang Chuan-kwang (Taiwan) would be gold medallist. At the finish, drained of strength, they collapsed against one another. The official winner was Johnson, but by 58 points only. Both men were studying at the same university, California at Los Angeles, and trained with the same coach.

" "

'One gold is better than two silvers.'

Mary Decker-Slaney (USA). In 1984, Decker was favourite for the 3000m but lost her only realistic chance of an Olympic gold medal through an untoward collision with Zola Budd (GB).

" "

'I'm going for three.'

Daley Thompson (GB), writing on a postcard during Moscow 1980 to American two-time decathlon victor Bob Mathias (1948 and 1952).

" "

'I didn't really expect to win one gold, let alone four.'

Fanny Blankers-Koen was the star woman track athlete at the 1948 London Games. Her first victory was in the 100m (2 August), and her further three were in the 80m hurdles (4 August), the 200m (6 August) and the 4×100m relay (7 August).

" "

'I'm not going to quit until I win five gold medals.'

Al Oerter (USA), discus specialist, who ultimately won four golds, one at each Games from 1956 to 1968. His first three children were each given one of his medals; the fourth is alleged to have said 'Go to Mexico, Daddy, and get me a goldy.'

" "

'It's like children, you don't have a favourite.'

British oarsman Sir Steve Redgrave won his fifth and last gold medal at Sydney in 2000, in the coxless four. His others had been in the coxless pair (Seoul 1988, Barcelona 1992, Atlanta 1996) and the coxed four (Los Angeles 1984).

" "

'Don't worry, I'll get another one.'

As reported in David Wallenchinsky's *The Complete Book of the Olympics* (Aurum, 1996), at his father's funeral, Carl Lewis laid the gold medal he had earned by winning the men's 100m in 1984 in his dead father's hands, saying 'I want you to have this because it was your favourite event'. Seeing his mother's astonishment, he quickly added the above soothing remark.

" "

'It is a silver, but for us it is more than 100 gold medals, it is more than even a gold mine.'

Mexico City 1968 Indonesian team coach Donald Pandiangan rejoices at his country's first ever Olympic medal, awarded in team archery.

" "

'Everyone else who finishes second is disappointed? I don't agree. The Olympics are about performance, doing the best you can do.'

Carl Lewis (USA) sprinted his way to victory five times at the Olympic Games (100m and 200m at Los Angeles in 1984; 100m at Seoul in 1988; 4×100m relay at Los Angeles in 1984 and Atlanta in 1996). He also won the long jump four consecutive times (1984–1996). Of these nine victories, six were in the United States on 'home ground'.

" "

'I got a bronze medal and I can't complain about that. The only African-American to get a medal in the Winter Olympics.'

Debi Thomas, bronze medallist in figure skating at the Calgary Winter Games in 1988. According to Willie Davenport, gold medallist in men's 110m hurdles at Mexico City in 1968, and himself, like Debi, a distinguished black American athlete, there was a myth that black people don't make the Winter Olympics.

" "

Rod Dixon (*sheepishly*): 'Is it enough?'

German doping official: 'For the gold medal, no, but for the bronze medal, it will do.'

Rod Dixon (New Zealand) had come third in the Munich 1972 men's 1500m and was struggling to provide a sufficient urine sample.

" "

'Fourth place, the worst possible position. You don't get a medal, but you still have to go through doping control.'

Flash quote by Henry Marsh (USA), fourth by 19 seconds in the Los Angeles 1984 men's 3000m steeplechase.

" "

'They placed the medal round my neck and played the national anthem. Nothing else in life will top that feeling. I came out of the ring and put that medal on my mother. After winning the gold medal, everything else is icing on the cake.'

American boxer Parnell Whittaker (USA), 1984 men's lightweight victor. Ben Johnson, too, won the gold medal 'for his mother' in 1988, but that story did not end happily.

" "

'When you stand on the victory stand, you must be able to ask yourself, "Did I *win* this medal?"'

Kenya's distance-runner Kip Keino, victor in the men's 1500m at Mexico City in 1968 and 3000m steeplechase at Munich in 1972, urges young athletes to think about and avoid 'performance-enhancing' drugs.

" "

'Let's have the medals off their necks!'

This angry reaction at the Los Angeles Games in 1984, from 'Jenny' Lang Ping, leader of the Chinese women's volleyball team, was justified. Facing the athletes' entrance to the Long Beach arena, the American organisers had crassly placed a huge TV screen with a freeze-frame of three USA team members prematurely wearing gold medals. Their hubris was punished; China won in straight sets.

" "

Very wise man: 'Are you happy?'

Harold Sakata: 'Sure.'

Very wise man: 'And you're proud of these silver trophies?'

Harold Sakata: 'Sure!'

Very wise man: 'Now let's see if you can eat them.'

Toshiyuki 'Harold' Sakata, better known as 'Oddjob' through his memorable role opposite Sean Connery in *Goldfinger*, was also an Olympic weightlifter (USA), and 1948 silver medallist at 410kg. The quotation recalls Jesse Owens's bitter words: 'People say that it was degrading for an Olympic champion to run against a horse, but what was I supposed to do? I had four gold medals but you can't eat four gold medals.'

" "

'If it's too complicated, then forget about the World Championship medals, but let's try to replace the Olympic medals at least.'

Oarsman and explorer James Cracknell (GB) had won two Olympic gold medals (2000 and 2004) in men's coxless fours. Here he was talking to IOC executive Denis Oswald, himself an Olympic coxed fours medallist, about trying to get them replaced after they were stolen. Happily, the medals were located by the dog of a neighbour, and the thief was caught and put in prison.

13
MONEY
SPEAKING

Money is one of those potentially lethal Greek inventions, like comedy and democracy. 'When money enters into sport,' said the historian of classical sport Ernest Gardner in 1930, 'corruption is sure to follow'; he undoubtedly got this one right. For Baron de Coubertin it was 'naive' to believe there was no bribery and corruption in the ancient Olympics, and in modern times, in 1920, when the Games of the VII Olympiad went into liquidation, the court's review observed that 'under pretext of supporting a great sporting event some people are conducting a lucrative financial scheme'. The spade was not called a spade until seventh International Olympic Committee (IOC) president Juan Antonio Samaranch, in the 1980s, asserted that holding the Games without commercialisation is 'an impossibility'; the Olympic Movement needs to be financially independent, with either the IOC or the local Organising Committee controlling the purse-strings. In 2000, French cynic Laurent Ruquier commented that we might expect Samaranch to get his gold medal for corruption as soon as Tahiti – average monthly temperature 29° Celsius – was awarded the Winter Games. Of Beijing 2008, the American advertiser Michael Wood said: 'You've never seen the Olympics in a market that has such domestic commercial scale'.

" "

'Talking about money is so vulgar.'

Mexico's Alpine skiing captain, photographer and pop singer Prince Hubertus Von Hohenlohe-Langenburg, being asked, in February 2010, about his country's Winter Games budget.

" "

'Water is all very well, *but* the glint of gold is like tawny fire in the night-time…'

The very first words of the very first *Olympic Cantata* by the Greek court poet Pindar, performed in 476 BC to celebrate the equestrian victory of the legendary tyrant of Sicily, Hieron. The truth that Pindar is pointing to, a very topical one, is that while water is essential for the health and survival of everyone, the glamour of the Olympic Games will always attract the wealthy few, whose ambition, like a bush fire, will devour everything in its path.

" "

'No person will be permitted to erect a Booth on the Hill, to sell any sort of beverage, without previously paying fifteen shillings to the Conductors of the Sports.'

The 1821 Regulations for the Cotswold Games.

" "

'…the profit that is made by a country – and a little country especially – that becomes the scene of the Olympic Games, will be certain, and of various kinds.'

Baron de Coubertin at an International Olympic Committee meeting in 1909.

" "

'There are few better ways [than the 1948 London Games] of making a net contribution to the balance of payments with so little offset in the form of imported materials.'

Herbert Morrison, deputy to Clement Attlee in the 1945 Labour administration. Morrison was of the opinion that the London 1948 Olympics would strengthen the national economy because the amounts received from the rest of the world from, for example, tourism would exceed the amount spent on imports. The only imported materials would be the athletes themselves.

" "

'Without the Olympics, Japan could not have climbed so far [and] so fast.'

Azuma Ryūtarō, mayor of the 1964 host city, Tokyo.

" "

'The Montreal Olympics can no more have a deficit than a man can have a baby.'

Lawyer and 1976 host city mayor Jean Drapeau speaking at a 1973 press conference. The man had a baby all right: the Montreal Games deficit was around US$1bn. In his candid survey *Inside the Olympics* (2006), Dick Pound – sixth in the 100m freestyle at Rome in 1960, and today a highly respected senior administrator in the IOC – called the Montreal Olympic Stadium 'hopelessly expensive, single-purpose and poorly located'.

" "

'The Olympics are slowly but surely being transformed into an advertisers' bonanza.'

English-Hungarian humorist George Mikes, in 1976.

" "

'There will never again be an official salad cream of the Olympic Games.'

Immortal words of Michael Payne, IOC Marketing Director, at Atlanta in 1996. They inadvertently revealed that Olympic marketing is prepared to handle anything and everything that can remotely be connected with Olympism, and to debar others from doing the same.

" "

'The Olympics are a corporate franchise that you buy with public money.'

Vancouver community activist Am Johal in 2010. For Andrew Jackson Young, diplomat and mainstay of the 1996 Atlanta Games bid team, the Olympics are 'the most significant generator of investment and private equity in the world today'.

" "

'The Olympics may cost London £9 billion and people are struggling all over the world, but this £9 billion is for a very good purpose. I know people in England are saying "Where's the benefit?" but they have to realise you can't see the benefit. It comes twenty or thirty years down the line in your grandchildren. Think back to 1948 when London hosted those fantastic Games at a difficult time. It was a gamble, but twenty years on it was worth it. They are history.'

Haile Gebrselassie (Ethiopia) twice men's 10,000m victor (1996 and 2000), and now a successful and compassionate businessman. 'You can't put a price on the results of an Olympics,' added Gebrselassie, 'and it's not all about getting your money back.'

" "

'…almost the entire population (for Athens boasts only about 130,000 people) was present at the Games. The poorest could afford to come, for prices ranged from 12 to 25 cents, according to the proximity of the sections to the royal seats.'

This was on day one of the first modern Games, in Athens in 1896, in the account of an observant American spectator, Burton Holmes. On day two there were fewer spectators; the excitement had worn off and grumbling about the ticket prices soon began. The contrast could not have been sharper with Marathon Day at the London 1908 Games, when the spectators inside the stadium numbered 90,000 or more, and black market ticket prices ranged from ten shillings to five gold sovereigns.

Amateur and pro

For most of its history, until the coming of the seventh president of the IOC, Juan Antonio Samaranch, in 1980, the modern Olympic Games has been plagued with the 'sham amateur'. Baron de Coubertin blamed the imperfect human condition for the mutating of the amateur Olympic athlete into a 'hired gladiator', the two things being 'incompatible'.

Since the amateur principle was, in the words of Theodor Lewald, president of the Berlin 1936 Games Organising Committee, 'a lofty and a sacred one', the IOC, with its stranglehold on the Games, went on turning a blind eye to 'perks'. (Spyros Louis, for example, the 23-year-old Greek water delivery boy who won the very first Olympic marathon in 1896, was immediately bombarded with free theatre tickets, free meals for life, a dove with a ribbon round its neck, and a rich lady's offer of either a large sum of money or a kiss – he opted for the kiss.) But it excluded from the Games any athlete 'tainted' by earning a living – of whatever kind and size – from sport. (Among the athletes whose careers this truncated was one of the very greatest, the American decathlete and 1912 gold medallist Jim Thorpe.) The issue rumbled on. Caspar Whitney, (the US author and president of the American Olympic Committee) before the First World War, had unforgivably called professionals 'vermin'. Avery Brundage (fifth president of the IOC), after the Second World War, called them 'performing monkeys'.

By 1968, that watershed year of twentieth century history with its student ferment and the Soviet invasion of Czechoslovakia, it was probably true in practice that, to quote the challenging words written in 1972 by the gutsy runner and winner of the Melbourne 1956 men's 3000m steeplechase, Christopher Brasher, 'the only amateurs in sport these days are those who are no good at it'. With reference to Montreal 1976, Olympic administrator and Melbourne single sculls bronze medallist Jack Kelly (USA) conceded that 'there are few world-class amateurs left in any sport' and defined the contemporary amateur as one who is paid in cash, the professional being paid by cheque.

Even at the start of the twenty-first century, a certain cachet still clung to amateurism that led lightweight boxer Amir Khan, silver medallist in 2004 at the age of seventeen, to wish to be World and Olympic Champion 'as an amateur'. Khan weighed up the advantages of remaining an amateur. These, in Britain, include shorter bourts, greater emphasis on technique, and access to the Amateur Boxing Association (ABA) network. Nevertheless, by 2008 he had turned professional.

" "

'There is professionalism of the richest hue prevalent in England; for where, in America, can a man bet on himself in pools like he can bet in England?'

Littlewoods may not have made the concept of the betting pool widely popular in Britain until 1923, but C. J. P. Lucas, St Louis head marathon official in 1904, had already come across it there.

" "

'When I needed a masseur I had to go out and pay for one. I had to pay for all my own equipment. What bugged me was that the people who came from overseas … were paid for by their governments, but we didn't get a penny for competing.'

Typically forthright comment from oarsman Bert Bushnell, gold medallist at the London 1948 Games.

" "

'This is a battle in which the future of sport and the Olympic Games is at stake.'

It wasn't, of course. Fifth IOC president Avery Brundage has a hissy fit about the professional ice hockey players at the St Moritz Winter Games in 1948. US vice president Walter Mondale overreacted almost identically about the United States Olympic Committee (USOC) vote in April 1980 on whether or not to take part in the Moscow Games: 'History holds its breath, for what is at stake here is no less than the future security of the civilized world.'

" "

'I run better when I am free.'

Steve Prefontaine (USA) long-distance runner and candidate for the Montreal 1976 Olympics, who was killed in a car crash in 1975.

'When I competed, no-one ever thought it would be possible to make money from something you enjoyed so much.'

The 'Dutch Housewife' Fanny Blankers-Koen, winner of three individual golds (100m, 200m, 80m hurdles) and one team gold (4×100m relay) at the London 1948 Games.

" "

'It's all a bit hypocritical. That bloke getting up on his legs and swearing blind they're amateurs.'

Italian discus thrower Adolfo Consolini, gold medallist in London 1948, speaking during the Rome Games in 1960.

" "

'I have never known an Olympic athlete who was an amateur.'

Shot-putter Parry O'Brien (USA), victor in 1952 and 1956, and worthy successor of Ralph Rose (USA), three-times gold medallist in shot put (1904, 1908, 1912).

" "

'In amateur sports you do it for the passion. You do it because you want to pursue Olympic gold.'

Jimmy Pedro (USA), two-time bronze medallist in judo (1996 and 2004).

" "

'So as an amateur Olympic competitor I loved criticism, because it made me better. But now as a professional I don't really know how to channel it or where to take it, so I don't take it quite as well.'

Figure skater Scott Hamilton (USA), victor at the 1984 Sarajevo Winter Games, who turned pro later that year. An invaluable objective view from an athlete who has competed in the Olympics both as an amateur and professional – thus bridging the divide.

" "

Matt Biondi (*striking a pose*): 'I'm going to Disneyland.'

Dick Pound: 'What are you doing?'

Biondi: 'I'm making a commercial.'

Swimmer Matt Biondi (USA) had just won the second of his three gold medals in 100m freestyle (1984, 1988 and 1992). Climbing out of the pool, he obliged his sponsors by delivering the above agreed catchphrase to camera. On hand was IOC vice-president Dick Pound, who saw to it that the tape was destroyed. Written in the fifth century BC, Pindar's words, 'The Games give their winners sweet ease for the rest of their lives', might have been tailor-made for Biondi, whose advice to Olympians was 'enjoy the journey, enjoy every moment, and quit worrying about winning and losing'.

" "

'We have to cut out all this amateur crap. It's phoney. We have to be openly professional, money on the table where everybody can see it.'

Multi-sport US athlete Carl Lewis was nine times Olympic victor. Four of his gold medals came in his first Games (Los Angeles 1984, 100m, 200m, 4×100m relay, long jump). Two were won at Seoul 1988 (100m, long jump), two more at Barcelona (long jump, 4×100m relay), and the last at Atlanta 1996 at the Centennial Games when Lewis had just passed his 35th birthday.

" "

'What will my country give me if I win 100 metres gold in Sydney? Tobago, probably.'

Ato Boldon of Trinidad and Tobago, men's 100m bronze medallist at Sydney 2000. Boldon's comment was humorous, but the Stockholm 1912 marathon winner, South Africa's Kenneth McArthur, was actually presented with a piece of land by his home town council on his victorious return.

And behind the Iron Curtain...

In Communist countries from 1948 to 1990, where sport was political action, the amateur versus professional issue was simply irrelevant. There are no 'amateurs' in the Marxist proletariet: only the working class doing its work. The Russian National Olympic Committee handbook of 2004 was continuing an earlier state of things when it announced that Olympic champions would have fixed presidential grants for life. In the old Soviet Union, sport was done either properly or not at all, and as USSR swimmer Birutė Statkevičiene, an unplaced competitor in the Munich 1972 women's 200m medley, explained for the benefit of Westerners: 'The Soviet Union was not a rich country. If you wanted to travel, sport was the best way.' It took the IOC some time to realise the awful truth:

" "

'We must face the fact that many of them are professionals.'

Sigfrid Edström, Swedish industrialist, sports administrator and fourth IOC President, in 1950 in a letter to the man who would two years later succeed him, Avery Brundage. The Soviet line was that all athletes were by historical necessity professional and entitled to accept pay. This philosophy spilled over the Soviet Union's borders, for example to Finland, whose national hero was the runner Paavo Nurmi. Thrice gold medallist at Antwerp in 1920 (10,000m, cross country both individual and team), then five times at Paris in 1924 (1500m, 5000m, cross country individual and team, and 3000m team), and finally once at Amsterdam in 1928 (10,000m), he was said by an Olympic official to have 'the lowest heart beat and the highest asking price of any athlete in the world'.

" "

'The Americans are prepared to bear the cost of the London Olympics, and guarantee food and sports equipment to ensure that sportsmen are from "politically reliable" countries. There is no doubt that the Olympic emblem will adorn not only belt clasps and ties, but also tins containing American Spam, under the mask of American pseudo-philanthropy.'

This lively passage (1947) was by a Soviet sports journalist named Sevidzh, on whom I have no further information.

" "

Leonid Litvinenko: 'Bruce, you gonna be Olympic champion!'

Bruce Jenner: 'Thanks.'

Litvinenko: '…Mmmm … Bruce, you gonna be millionaire?'

Jenner: (*chuckles*)

Leonid Litvinenko (USSR) and Bruce Jenner (USA), respectively seventh and first in the Moscow decathlon, as reported in Wallenchinsky's *The Complete Book of the Olympics* (Aurun, 1996).

" "

'We need the Olympic Games to feed and clothe our children.'

Chen Xitong, Secretary of the Chinese Communist Party, interviewed in 2008 ahead of the Beijing Games. In the complex manoeuvres of Beijing politics, Chen, an opponent of the Tiananmen Square protests in 1989, had been removed from his post as the city's mayor during an anti-corruption drive in 1995. Jailed in 1998, he was rehabilitated in 2006 in nice time to spearhead the Olympic campaign.

14
NATIONALISM

As Spencer Kyle, Scotland's Olympic hope in the Sydney 2000 men's tennis, remarked, 'you don't get to choose where you are born'. The 1908 Official Report recognised a special Olympic sense of the word 'nation', but some have felt that nationalistic elements should be eliminated from the Games altogether, since a central item in Olympism is its faith in the worldwide, the purely human. Thus for the victory ceremony, British runner and gold medallist at Melbourne 1956, Chris Brasher would far rather have had just the Olympic anthem and flag than 'the present jingoistic affair'. Interviewed for an evening newspaper, Sir Tom Stoppard, the playwright, branded the Olympics 'the voice of nationalist triumphalism'.

" "

'I don't want to attach an absurd importance to athletics, but, seriously, it seems to me that international contests do provide a sort of international rivalry that is sane and healthy and desirable. Is it so fantastic to believe that [this] will help ...

in breaking up the absurd fabric of routine thinking on which the present system of international relations rests?'

From a 1912 article by Philip Noel-Baker (GB), 1920 silver medallist at 1500m, and team manager at the 1920 and 1924 Games; he was also an internationalist, prime mover in the League of Nations and a pacifist.

" "

'Why do you have to wear the uniform of your country? Why do they play the national anthems? Why do we have to beat the Russians? Why do the East Germans want to beat the West Germans? Why can't everybody wear the same colors but wear numbers to tell them apart? What happened to the Olympic ideal of man against man?'

Black US athlete John Carlos, bronze medallist in the 200m in his first appearance as Olympic competitor, at Mexico City in 1968. It is not this for which he is remembered, however, but for his associated 'political' act, amid the charged atmosphere of summer 1968, with its student protests. Carlos had come third in the race; the winner was his fellow black athlete Tommie Smith. At the award ceremony, standing on the podium after receiving their medals, both men gave the raised-fist Black Power salute. The gesture sparked off huge controversy in the States and elsewhere. The words quoted were Carlos's plaintive reply soon after, under questioning from his critics.

" "

'I see that your internationalism … does not kill national spirit – it strengthens it.'

The French writer and royalist politician Charles Maurras, present in Athens 1896, points out to Baron de Coubertin a flaw in the Olympic Movement.

" "

'Governments insist on treating the Olympics as a political power game, an earnest display of national virility on which vast fortunes are spent.'

British humorist William Davis writing in 1976 at the time of the Montreal Olympics.

" "

'Flags are essentially political emblems which divide rather than unite.'

Sixth IOC president Lord Killanin (Ireland) is talking, in his memoirs *My Olympic Years* (1983), about emblems on blazer pockets. As a representative of a divided Ireland, he was all too familiar with this kind of problem.

" "

'A group of excited and gesticulating Frenchmen who, not content with making themselves ridiculous ... also refused to allow anyone in their proximity to get a view of the fight...'

The British Olympic Committee's report in the Paris 1924 Games describes the middleweight final between two British competitors: Henry Mallin, a London policeman, and John Elliott. The cause of the uproar was that, after the previous round, Roger Brousse (France), had been eliminated for leaving visible bite-marks on Mallin.

" "

'Finland won.'

In the quarter-final of the 1912 Stockholm football tournament, Finland beat Russia before an audience of 300. Finland was still a Russian subject province, so the victors' flag was accompanied by the Russian imperial eagle. However, the officials succeeded in 'cancelling' the eagle with a pennant carrying the single word 'Suomi' ('Finland') in bold relief.

" "

'He made our flag to float
Over dead and departed Mussolini's head
Then O then
Abebe led and Mamo came behind
Ethiopia led and Kenya came behind
He made us friends among nations...'

The *Ethiopian Herald*, in 1973, printed this song of triumph and mourning for the recently dead Abebe Bikila (Ethiopia), who won the 1960 marathon in Rome with compatriot Mamo Wolde coming second. Bikila's compatriot Miruts Yifter, double gold medallist at Moscow in 1980 in the 5000m and the 10,000m, said when interviewed in 1997: 'Throughout my life I was running for the people of Ethiopia and for my beloved flag.'

" "

'When I put on this vest, I feel no pain.'

For Hendrick Ramaala (South Africa), who finished 12th at Sydney 2000 in the marathon, wearing his country's colours blotted out all fatigue.

" "

'…to compete for my country and my people and to receive the support of the entire Cuban society, to carry my flag in whatever competition I was in, the Olympic Games…'

Alberto Juantorena (Cuba), winner of the 400m at Montreal in 1976, tells of his pride at representing his country.

" "

'This is not *my* gold medal! This is the [Turkish] *people's* gold medal!'

Weightlifter Naim Suleymoğlu (Turkey), after the first of his two victories in men's featherweight (1988, 1992), speaking on TV after returning home.

" "

'I did it automatically, for my country.'

At Seoul 1988, after public protests about anti-host country bias, South Korean Olympic security guard S. L. Yoon joined in a general punch-up when local boxer Byun Jong-Il (bantamweight) controversially lost his second-round bout.

" "

'Under protest.'

The unofficial sign which Taiwan's placard-bearer flashed when passing the Presidential Box during the Opening Ceremony at Rome in 1960. Taiwan, a small island off the south-east coast of mainland China, became the refuge of the country's Nationalists when eventually defeated by Mao Zedong's Chinese Communist forces in 1949. So that the People's Republic of China could make its Olympic debut, the IOC had pressured Taiwan to parade in under the colonial designation 'Formosa'.

" "

'Why did Columbus ever discover your unbeatable country?'

Greek prime minister Theodoros Deligiannis, turning to America's official representative after the fourth US victory at the 1896 Athens Games.

" "

'One should look in the American sportsman not for the light vices of vain or sensual loungers, but for the solid vices of statesmen and fanatics, for the sins of men inflamed by patriotism or religion. He cannot shake hands after the fight; he feels towards his conqueror as a man towards the invader who has robbed him of his God.'

Virtually from the start of the London 1908 Games, the air was thick with British and American journalists', athletes' and officials' accusations and counter-accusations (see Preface). This weighty shot in the cannonade was fired by the towering English Catholic writer G. K. Chesterton.

" "

'The Americans seem to think they can bring their own ideas of sport over here and enforce them.'

A reporter for the London *Sportsman*, 1908. The US athletes in the first Games had regarded themselves, and had been regarded, as on a goodwill mission and as an advertisement for the American type; for fair play and for give and take. This was pungently expressed by the Irish-American humorist Peter Finley Dunne: 'These boys that you see hoppin' around th' thrack arre the rile represintive Amurricans. They are our ambassadurs, not the lordhs ye see makin' a ginuflixion before th' king'. However, at Stockholm in 1912 the mission became (according to the official report) 'an unparallelled athletic invasion'.

" "

'At the Olympics, you're there to do a job. I feel you should take it seriously. You should be respectful. You are putting on the red, white, and blue and going out there to perform for your country.'

Oklahoma's Olympic double victor in gymnastics (team and balance beam) at Atlanta 1996, Shannon Miller, competed in her first Olympics at Barcelona in 1992, winning two silvers (all-around, balance beam) and three bronzes (team, uneven bars, floor).

" "

**'To make America the greatest is my goal,
So I beat the Russian and I beat the Pole.'**

Cassius Clay, later the great Mohammed Ali, men's light heavyweight champion in Rome 1960, with one of his short rhymed jabs from *How Cassius Took Rome.*

" "

'I always thought it was a lot of hogwash to say that you ran for your flag and your country. I was just out there to beat the guy beside me.'

Canada's Percy Williams, victor at Amsterdam 1928 in the 100m and 200m, interviewed five weeks after his triumphs.

" "

'Waving the flag at the 1976 Olympics wasn't my idea. It was too much apple pie and ice cream. Not that I don't love my country, but I felt it was my victory up there, I put all the time into it...'

Bruce Jenner (USA), decathlon victor at Montreal, in a CBS interview, July 1980.

'Every day [Finns] would like a new world record. But I don't care. I'm running only for the Olympic Games.'

Finnish police officer Lasse Virén took part in the Munich 1972 Games only a year after his international debut, winning golds at 5000m and 10,000m, a feat he was to repeat at Montreal in 1976. Interviewed in 1977, this enigmatic athlete placed Olympic victory above 'a new world record' and national glory.

" "

'Even if I'm not the Finnish champion, at least I've won the Olympics.'

Pauli Nevala (Finland), Rome 1964 men's javelin gold medallist.

15

OLYMPIASTADION 1936

If one particular Games marks the true start of the modern international Olympics it is not Athens 1896, but Berlin 1936. For the first time, the power of spectacle and propaganda were properly appreciated; host cities Amsterdam in 1928 and Los Angeles in 1932 had got less than halfway.

The International Olympic Committee could never have dreamt that it would have to cooperate with hard-line fascism when Berlin was awarded the Games in April 1931. The fateful elections that placed Adolf Hitler in power took place only in 1932, and he was persuaded, after initial disdain, of the Games' usefulness as a propaganda tool. A whole Olympic ideology and mythology was subsequently manufactured.

There were protests from the European and American Left. In France, the incoming premier was Léon Blum, whose electoral promises had included non-participation in the Games. A Communist deputy in the French parliament spelt out the position without mincing words.

" "

'Go to Berlin, and you accept a kind of pact with the torturers; you shackle the irons to the victims' legs; and drown their cries by chanting a hymn of praise to Sport and the Reichmaster.'

But attending the Berlin Games was fashionable. The Conservative MP 'Chips' Channon and his wife Honor, of the Guinness family, took Goering or Goebbels in their stride (so the English political observer Harold Nicolson wrote in his diary), relishing 'the champagne-like influence of Ribbentrop' and of the youthful German nobility. American journalist William Shirer conceded, with alarm, a propaganda victory: not only had the Nazis run the Games more lavishly than ever before, which drew athletes, but they had put up a very good front for general visitors, especially big businessmen. Returning from the Games, future International Olympic Committee (IOC) president Avery Brundage told a Madison Square Garden audience at his German Day speech on 4 October: 'We can learn much from Germany.'

" ,,

'It is too bad that the American Jews are so active and cause us so much trouble. It is impossible for our German friends to carry on the expensive preparations for the Olympic Games if all this unrest prevails.'

The IOC's fourth president Sigfrid Edström in a letter, dated 12 April 1933, to his friend Avery Brundage. In his 1935 *Final Report* to the American Olympic Committee, Brundage, taking his standard line, would say, indefensibly, that politics had no place in sport, and that 'certain Jews' needed to understand that they could not use the Games 'as a weapon in their boycott against the Nazis'.

" ,,

'I believe that for America to participate in the Olympics in Germany means giving American moral and financial support to the Nazi regime, which is opposed to all that Americans hold dearest.'

Judge Jeremiah Mahoney (USA), Amateur Athletic Union president, led liberal protests in 1934–5. The Roman Catholic publication *The Commonweal*, with which Mahoney was associated, referred on 8 November 1935 to the 'anti-Christian Nazi doctrine of youth'.

Ernest Jahncke (USA), then a member of the IOC was expelled for his opposition to the Berlin Games.

" "

'Never before has there been a propaganda campaign to match that of the [Berlin] Olympic Games ... Tourism is a vital weapon in Germany's efforts to re-establish her rank.'

This memorandum was written by Nazi propaganda minister Joseph Goebbels. His formula was to be 'more charming than the Parisians; more easygoing than the Viennese; more vivacious than the Romans; more cosmopolitan than London; and more practical than New York.'

" "

'...the greatest and most glorious athletic festival ever conducted – the most spectacular and colossal of all time ... The 1936 Olympic Games were removed from their normal plane and lifted to a dazzling precedent which probably no country can hope to follow.'

Avery Brundage, IOC president (1952–1972). Taking his cue from de Coubertin, Theodor Lewald (president of the 1936 Organising Committee) spoke of 'a stately, brilliant and chivalrous festival ... a veritable *Ver sacrum*, a sacred springtime of all peoples.'

" "

'This Games has been just what I wanted it to be ... In Berlin, people thrilled to a concept which, though we are no longer in a position to judge it, was that same passionate stimulant that I am constantly looking for ... As for the technical side, that was done with all the care that could be wished, nor can the Germans be accused of any lack of sporting loyalty. This being so, can you really expect me to renege on the celebrations of the Eleventh Olympiad? For this glorification of the Nazi regime was also the emotional shock that permitted the Games to develop as tremendously as they have done.'

An article by de Coubertin in September 1936.

" "

'Berlin was awe-inspiring. We were greeted at the station by brass bands and Hitler Youth. You couldn't help being impressed by the Teutonic efficiency. The shop assistants greeted us with a Nazi salute and "Guten Morgen. Heil Hitler". So I did a Girl Guide salute and said "Heil King George".'

Dorothy Tyler MBE, British high-jump silver medallist at Berlin in 1936 and again, after the war, at London in 1948.

" "

Interviewer: 'How did those dirty Nazis treat you?' Archie Williams: 'I didn't see any *dirty* Nazis, just a lot of nice German people. And I didn't have to sit in the back of the bus over there.'

As Archie Williams (USA), Berlin victor at 400m, would have had to do in 1936 back home, being African-American.

" "

'I had such fun! I enjoyed the parties, the "Heil Hitlers", the uniforms, the flags … Goering was fun. He had a good personality. So did the one with the club foot.'

The one with the club foot was Dr Goebbels. Here, revelling in Berlin's atmosphere was the socialite swimmer and 'All American Girl' Eleanor Holm Jarrett, 100m backstroke gold medallist at Los Angeles in 1932 (she did not compete in 1936).

" "

'Hitler comes in and gives me the Nazi salute. I gave him a good old Missouri handshake. Immediately Hitler goes for the jugular. He gets a hold of my fanny, and begins to squeeze and pinch me up, and he said, "You're a true Aryan type. You should be running for Germany". So after he gave me the once-over and a full massage, he asked me if I'd like to spend the weekend at Berchtesgaden.'

Six-feet-tall brunette high school girl Helen Stephens (USA), 1936 victor in the 100m. She did not appreciate the Führer's advances.

'I wanted no part of politics. And I wasn't in Berlin to compete against any one athlete. The purpose of the Olympics, anyway, was to do your best. As I'd learned long ago from Charles Riley [coach], the only victory that counts is the one over yourself.'

Jesse Owens (USA), as reported by Tony Gentry in his biography *Champion Athlete* (1990). Owens's brilliance as a sprinter at the 1936 Berlin Games, with four golds to his name (100m, 200m, 4×100m team relay), captivated the spectators and made nonsense of Nazi racial theories.

" "

'We got to be great friends, Hitler or no Hitler.'

Jesse Owens. His friend – whom the *New York Times* correspondent at Berlin in 1936, Arthur Daley described as 'blond, lean and blue-eyed, a walking advertisement for Hitler's ideal' – was Luz Long, the German men's long jump silver medallist in Berlin. Owens's feelings of affection overflowed when Long congratulated him on his victory in the long jump, and he noted Long's great moral courage in befriending him, a black American, before Hitler's very eyes. Long would die aged 30, fighting on the Eastern Front.

" "

'He waved at me and I waved back. I think it was bad taste to criticize "the man of the hour" in another country.'

Jesse Owens's own statement, reported by United Press with the comment 'As for Adolf Hitler, Owens had nothing but kind words'.

" "

'Hitler wouldn't shake my hand either.'

Black-American sprinter, Archie T. Williams, Berlin victor in the 400m, said the above flippantly, when asked about Hitler's (reported) refusal to shake Jesse Owens's hand, a gesture forbidden in any case by protocol.

   P. G. Wodehouse was ahead of his time in debunking the Berlin Games in *Lord Emsworth and Others* (1937), with barbed references to 'moustaches', 'intense competition' and the 'amateur sport which has made us Englishmen what we are'. Otherwise hindsight was needed to see the Games for what they were, after the end of the Second World War, when the glamour had worn off.

" "

'The Games had grown in political importance until the Germans overstepped all bounds of sportsmanship with a vulgar display, calculated to impress visitors not so much with their prowess as with their military efficiency.'

British journalist John Macadam, looking back at the Berlin 1936 Games at the time of the London 1948 Games. Sir Arthur Elvin stated: 'The approach is quite different from the 1936 Berlin Games. We want to see the best men win, no matter where they come from or who they represent'.

" "

'The Nuremberg Games were designed to promote a human monoculture: the Olympic Games are a celebration of complete failure by them – and many others. They tell us … about the boggling biodiversity of the human species.'

Times chief sports writer Simon Barnes in a 2008 article. For Netherlands swimmer and 1936 Olympic triple gold medallist Rie Mastenbroek similarly, the Berlin Games produced 'not a sausage' ('*geen millemoer*').

16
ORIGINS

'It is not generally known ... that the far-famed Games of Ancient Greece drew [their] inspiration from the still more ancient Games in Ireland.'

Many have tried and failed to appropriate the origin of the Olympic Games. Here, Irish historian T. H. Nally, in 1920, lays claim to them. Lebanese historian Labib Boutros, in 1981, proposed that the Games originated in Syria in Phoenician times, at Amrit, 7km south of Tartous.

" "

'Olympia was not a city, it was a shrine ... It is something quite other, transcendent.'

Demetrios Vikélas (Greece), first president of the IOC writing for his friend the Marquis Queux de Saint-Hilaire in 1885.

" "

'Life is like the showpiece of the Olympic Games. Some go there to take part. Others go there for business purposes.

But the Wise attend them only to see what goes on. So too in human life, some are slaves to glory, some to love and money. But the Wise seek there naught but Truth.'

Words attributed to the sixth-century BC Greek mathematician and esoteric thinker Pythagoras by Jean Mallinger, a French jurist.

" "

Messenger (*running in to the Agora*): Rejoice, Athenians! We've won! (*collapses and dies*).

Authentic? The message of the first-ever marathon runner as he arrives, in the best traditions of Greek tragedy, to report to the anxious citizens of Athens the victory against the Persian invader in 490 BC.

The Jewish king Hordos (40–4 BC) (the Herod of the Christmas story) was a fan of Greek culture as well as a ruthless ruler and a crack archer and rider. On his way to Rome, either in 12 or 8 BC, he stopped off at Olympia for long enough to preside over the Games, which had dwindled almost to nothing because their Greek organisers had run out of money (what's new?). Hordos optimistically made them a massive grant so that the memory of his visit should remain green forever. Meanwhile he was building impressive sports and entertainment venues in his own land of Judea: the pool at the city named after him, Herodium, was about double the size of a modern Olympic pool.

" "

'Let there be no place available to non-believers in which to celebrate their rituals.'

The writing was on the wall for the Olympic Games when this decree was issued in AD 391 by the successful general of the East Romans, Theodosios I, a thorough and on occasion ruthless emperor. The decree slotted into his long campaign to eliminate pagan practices, the Olympics being only one small item. The Games likely ceased with the end of the 293rd Olympiad in AD 393, and the temples at Olympia, having no potential for rededication, were wrecked or recycled soon after.

" "

'As I gazed upon the coast of Elis, not many miles from the sacred place in which the Olympic Games, the nurse of Grecian virtue and enterprise, were celebrated, the melancholy reflection of its departed glory succeeded the joy I at first felt.'

The English traveller in Eastern lands, Thomas Watkins, in 1792.

" "

'Faded is Thebes and faded is Athens; no longer do weapons Sound at Olympia now, or the golden chariots of sportstrife...'

The German lyric poet Friedrich Hölderlin, in *Brot und Wein* (1801).

" "

'We left at eight that glorious morning. We kept to the right bank of the Alpheus, and the mountains, with their many fine specimens of spruce and pine, gradually gave way to a wide valley. After about an hour's journey the side of the mountain we were going along made a sort of cup that broadened into a plain on the edges of which, here and there, were wooded knolls. Two trenches were the evidence of the excavations by the French Mission. Nothing was left of ancient Olympia but the remains of great walls, some massive upturned stones, and the fluted base of a column, of colossal size.'

Olympia as seen by the French novelist, Gustave Flaubert, in 1850. Excavation was renewed in 1936, enabling Hitler to declare that 'a sacred centre of ancient culture will thus be made available to present-day humanity'.

17
OVERCOMING ADVERSITY

'I'm not disabled. I just don't have any legs.'

Paralympic victor Oscar Pistorius (South Africa) interviewed in 2010. With the use of his carbon-fibre artificial limbs, Pistorius won four Paralympic golds in class T44 track events (100m at Athens 2004 and Beijing 2008; 200m and 400m at Beijing 2008). Indeed there is some fear in that he may be 'faster' than able-bodied runners.

" "

'How far is far, how high is high? We'll never know until we try.'

From 'Possibilities', the theme song of the California Special Olympics (founded 1969). It reworks a phrase of the US sprinter Wilma Rudolph (3 golds at Rome 1960, in 100m, 200m, 4×100m relay). 'There's no goal too far, no mountain too high'.

" "

'Part of what the Special Olympics is trying to do is break down stereotypes that still exist in people. There is still a lot of fear.'

The Special Olympics and the Paralympic games are similar in that both are recognised by the IOC; different in that the former is for athletes with intellectual disabilities, the latter is for elite athletes from six specific disability groups. Maria Shriver (USA) is a publicist for both and the daughter of the late Eunice Shriver, who founded the Special Olympics, sister of president John F. Kennedy.

" "

'The Olympic Games are dealt with by the Assembly [the Lower House of the French Parliament], the Paralympics are left to the Senate [the Upper, more elderly House].'

The Assembly is the French Parliament's Lower Chamber; the Senate, its Upper and more elderly Chamber. Jean-Louis Debré, French Gaullist politician and president of the Constitutional Council, uttered this grossly un-PC bon mot after a reception in 2005 and was roundly condemned.

" "

'The Australians love sport and will applaud achievement no matter what sport it is, and that includes disabilities. I was quite blown away by their attitude and I think it marks a step change.'

Linda Mitchell, chief physio to Britain's Athens 2004 Paralympics squad, and wife of wheelchair tennis 2012 entrant Peter Norfolk.

" "

'Part of my preparations now is to throw up before each event.'

Tanni Grey-Thompson (now Baroness Grey-Thompson), one of Britain's greatest Paralympic competitors, whose eleven gold medals, at 100m and 800m, span the years 1992–2004. Here she triumphs over nerves and the body with a spirited sense of humour.

" "

'It was quite late in the evening when they said I had to be offloaded from the bus to collect my medal. It was totally surprising. At that stage I didn't even know it was the gold until I was wheeled on to the winners' platform.'

Margaret Maughan, multiple Paralympic archery gold medallist, going to her medal ceremony at the still rather experimental first Paralympics, Rome 1960.

18
PEOPLE

'[I] felt like a condemned man feels just before going to the scaffold.'

Harold Abrahams (GB), Paris 1924 double victor in the men's 100m and relay, awaited the 100m final for some four hours.

" "

'...that blazing day in Seoul, the light hurting your eyes and the yellow-eyed, shaven-head human bullet taking the stage to turn the world upside-down. And then, 9.79 seconds later, he had finished, the last two strides floating, celebrating, finger pointing to the skies. Ben Johnson had won the 100 metres, redefining our understanding of human potential.'

The image of US sprinter Ben Johnson at Los Angeles in 1984, indelibly impressed on Simon Barnes at the time. Another British sports writer, Paul Hayward, saw Johnson very differently: his 'yellow-eyed charge down the 100 metre track in Seoul was the ultimate demonstration of drug-induced depravity in sport'.

" "

'Getting to know athletes from all over the planet is a big part of the Olympic experience … if you're isolated from the heart of the Games, the Olympics become just another competition.'

Mary Lou Retton (USA), 1984 gymnastics all-around gold medallist.

" "

Journalist: 'How come you run so fast?'

Wilma Rudolph: 'Man, in my family you had to run fast if you wanted to eat.'

Wilma Rudolph (USA), three-times gold medallist in 1960 (100m, 200m and 4×100m relay).

" "

'He strode along with a smoothness and an indifference to his awful task that left us spellbound.'

The body movement of the Finnish distance runner Paavo Nurmi while running his Olympic gold medal in the 5000m at Paris in 1924, as described by British journalist Ben Bennison.

" "

'Biwott leaped the water jump as though he thought crocodiles were swimming in it.'

Amos Biwott, Kenyan 3000m steeplechase victor at Mexico City in 1968, described by *Runner's World* commentator Joe Henderson.

" "

'Mrs Blankers-Koen from Holland, with her orange shorts and her fair floating hair, strode home to victory with all the irresistible surge of the great men sprinters, and stealing half their thunder.'

The Times salutes the great Dutch runner's performance in London 1948.

'It came like electricity, it came from every fibre, from his fingertips to his toes. It came as broad waters come through a gorge. He called on it all.'

New Zealand sports writer Norman Harris magnificently portrays New Zealand runner Jack Lovelock's final kick-thrust to claim a legendary victory in the 1936 Berlin 1500m.

" "

'Well, good-bye, Billy.'

Athens 1906 marathon victor William John Sherring (Canada), spurting away after three miles alongside William Frank (USA) (who won bronze) at the 18th mile.

" "

'A smallish man in crimson knickers and a crimson handkerchief tied around his head tottered onto the track with his legs almost giving way under him and apparently blind ... It really was a wonderful sight and, although extremely painful, I am very glad I saw it. Hayes and Dorando were really magnificent, their pluck was simply marvellous.'

Vera Cox, then a 14-year-old London schoolgirl, had just seen Dorando Pietri's famous marathon in 1908, and was writing home to her parents.

" "

King Gustav Of Sweden: 'Sir, you are the greatest athlete in the world.'

Jim Thorpe (*awkwardly*): 'Thanks, King.'

Authentic, I think, from a 1912 medal ceremony as reported in *Time* magazine, 6th of April, 1953. Jim Thorpe (USA) specialised in pentathlon and decathlon. *Herald Tribune* journalist Walter Wellesley 'Red' Smith called Thorpe 'the greatest athlete of his time, maybe the greatest of any time in any land'. In 1912 Thorpe, falling foul of the amateur clause, was stripped of his Stockholm pentathlon and decathlon gold medals; 'no other Olympian ever got such a rough deal' (commented sports historian Robert Quercetani). The IOC restored the medals in 1983, by which time Thorpe had already died, demoralised and a pauper.

" "

Emil Zátopek (*labouring*): 'Isn't the pace too fast?'

Jim Peters (*joking*): 'No, it's too slow.'

Emil Zátopek: 'You say, too slow? Are you sure the pace is too slow?'

In the early stages of his maiden marathon at Helsinki in 1952, Zátopek was alongside the British favourite, Jim Peters. The Czech was already tired and Peters was running 'like he could do this for ever'. The above exchange took place. But Peters's pace was his undoing; eventually the heat overcame him and he didn't finish. Zátopek, however, spurted forward, keeping his lead to win in record time.

" "

'I had a lot of fun jumping the hurdles, like an animal – my style is not good.'

Kenyan distance runner Kip Keino, to journalists shortly after his victory in the 3000m steeplechase at Munich in 1972.

" "

'I said to myself, "Well, you've run in the semi-finals and equalled the Olympic record; Bob, you're really getting the hang of it!"'

Bob Tisdall (Ireland), 1932 men's 400m hurdles victor and eighth in the decathlon. After his record run, Tisdall is rumoured to have celebrated by downing a whole bottle of champagne.

" "

'…a strapping, wholesome, fun-loving young creature, with muscles of steel and a great chuckle in her throat…'

Description of Gertrude Ederle (USA) contained within the *Literary Digest*, 1924 bronze medallist at age 17 in 110m and 400m freestyle, and first female English Channel swimmer. Having gone overboard with this macho description of her in 1924, the *Literary Digest*, in a fine show of political correctness, smoothed her down in 1926 to 'the bob-haired daughter of the Jazz Age'.

" "

'I could wrestle with you, and sit on you too!'

Prince George of the Hellenes, Greece, to an official entrant in Athens 1896. At the weightlifting, the prince is said to have picked up a dumb-bell that one of the contestants could barely lift, and nonchalantly handed it to him.

" "

'Για την Ελλάδα, ρε γαμώτο!'

'[I did it] for Greece, for God's sake!'

Flash quote by Voula Patoulidou, about the gold medal she had just won in the women's 100m hurdles at Barcelona 1992. It is now a common catchphrase among all patriotic Greeks.

" "

'They were men of between twenty and thirty, of middling height, lean, bony, very athletic-looking and well-trained, moving with the grace of gymnasts, very noticeably agile and elegant, too much so almost.'

The German Olympic soccer team, as portrayed in the 1900 Official Report.

Officials

Despite the complexities of organising the Olympic Games in the twenty-first century, the Athens' Crown Prince Constantine believed the aim was is still to show athletes and spectators the 'hearty and flawless hospitality' that was on offer in 1896. The reputation of a Games stands or falls by its officials. Keeping them in line is the International Olympic Committee (IOC), many of whom are ex-athletes.

" "

'Everything fixed. You have Olympic Games.'

A cablegram sent in 1903 by Michel Le Grave, one of the Commissioner's of the 1900 Paris Expo, which had included an athletics meeting, not billed as the Olympic Games. Le Grave, after consultation with the International Olympic Committee, was belatedly reassuring the candidate host city, St Louis (Missouri), that they had been officially chosen. This procedure strikes one as the reverse of transparent.

" "

'The Games is like a huge mobile sculpture, with wheels and pulleys, levers and cogs. It isn't till you turn the thing on that you even know if all the bits will move together as they're meant to.'

François Carrard, Swiss lawyer and IOC director-general in an interview in *Big Issue Australia,* 17th September 2010.

" "

'When I think of the anonymous attacks on the IOC, the traps and obstacles that cabals and envious fanatics have placed in its path over the last fourteen years...'

Baron de Coubertin speaking at the 1908 official banquet for Games officials.

" "

XYZ: Are we really to believe that it is solely the Olympic Committee which binds these disparate entities [the nations of the world] together? ... But ... perhaps the group of administrators, CEOs and NGO chairs are actually Illuminati, tending the strings of worldwide domination as carefully as the hedges of the Olympic parks and stadia.

ABC: ...You don't know the half. How could you? Yes, the Olympics is a conspiracy. Of course it is. It is a worldwide cooperative organization of spectacular entertainment ... the globe over. It has no noble purposes, and it couldn't have one if it wanted to.

Blogspot: *fƆutn●Jones* (Feuilleton Jones) in 2000. British Columbia's Court of Appeal, in 2009, rejected the case for women's ski jumping as an Olympic discipline in 2010, prompting a Canadian blogger, 'Digital Citizen', to ask, 'Are the IOC that powerful they could just go in and trump the law of the land?', and to conclude that the Olympic Charter had priority over the Canadian Charter of Rights.

IOC presidents

'...one of the purest and noblest figures in the Greek world today. Nobody ever had a warmer heart, or more generous intentions, or truer dedication. And there was none who worked as hard and as willingly as Vikelas, to do away with the obstacles to the holding of the Olympic Games in Athens. Vikelas was the very incarnation of the Hellenic spirit...'

Baron de Coubertin's epitaph for Demetrios Vikélas of Greece (1835–1908), lawyer and writer, first IOC president, prime mover of Athens' 1896 Olympic Games. In early 1895, Vikélas, a diplomat in all but name, was writing as many as three letters a week from Athens to de Coubertin in Paris. Praising his unstinting energy, the Baron acknowledged that Vikélas was winning over many Greek government and opposition politicians to the concept of an Athenian Games by asking them to put patriotism above economics. De Coubertin's fulsome tribute is in stark contrast to his sidelining of Vikélas once the Olympics were prospering in the twentieth century.

" "

'The Winter Olympics have ended without anyone's drawing a knife and without anyone tossing a domick [rock] at Avery Brundage's balding pate.'

Leading American columnist Arthur Daley, in 1948. 'Strait-laced' Avery Brundage, as *Time International* called him, was the fifth IOC president. Red Smith termed him 'the greatest practising patsy ... of this century': *Mirriam-Webster* defines a 'patsy' as 'a person who is easily manipulated or victimised'. At Mexico City in 1968, the US gold medallist in the 200m, Tommie Smith told reporters, 'I don't want Brundage presenting me no medals.'

'No monarch ever held sway over such a vast expanse of territory [as I do].'

Avery Brundage, addressing the IOC's 57th session in 1960.

" "

'[Myles na Gopaleen] once sent me a label bearing the name of the Russian ship, the M.V. *Mikhail Kallinin*, on which a friend of his had been travelling – a favour I was later to put to good use when speeches were required of me during the Olympic Games in Moscow.'

'Myles na Gopaleen' was the Irish humorist Flann O'Brien, and the speaker was Michael Lord Killanin, the sixth IOC president, also a man with a sense of humour. The name on the label, Mikhail Kallinin, was what 'Michael Killanin' might very well become, at the Moscow Games in 1980, when the IOC president and his Russian friends had had a few vodkas.

" "

'It smacked of the retirement of the Sun King, with medals struck, obsequious speeches, photo ops with Moscow mayor Yuri Luzhkov, galas and banquets that, in the end, became offensive.'

The last banquet of Juan Antonio Samaranch's reign as IOC president, 2001, is here described by former IOC vice-president Dick Pound in his memoirs, *Inside the Olympics* (2004).

" "

'I find it hard to put up with people that build palaces of words.'

Gianna Angelopoulos, president of the Athens 2004 Organising Committee.

" "

'Athletes need coaches, but the roster of Olympic participants is bloated with bureaucrats and hangers-on.'

The verdict of Olympic encyclopaedist David Wallechinescky in his massive and indispensable tome *The Complete Book of the Summer Olympics,* regularly updated.

'The Reich Ministry of the Interior ordered the creation of a special Police Commanding Staff for the XIth Olympiad.'

The policing of the Games at Berlin in 1936 enabled techniques of supervision to be tried out. In 1896 public order had been entrusted to 'agents of the stadium' (gendarmes); London 1908 brought in 'extra police supervision'; in 2004 a mid-air presence that we grew to be rather fond of was the telecommunications spy zeppelin. Security has been, and remains, a major Olympic preoccupation.

" "

'Everybody remembers from the "Stadium-days" how the little, sun-burned, blue and grey boys ran about, selling programmes and fans, letting out cushions, procuring water, wiping the perspiration from the bodies of wrestlers, recalling fainting ladies to consciousness, or going home to the dwellings of private individuals, in order, in accordance with the directions of the owners, to find pocket-books or a bunch of keys lying in the depths of some secret drawer, the position of which had been told them.'

The report on the 1912 Stolkholm Games brings vividly to life the Boy Scouts who made themselves useful as volunteers. Scouting was very new; it had made its appearance only five years before.

" "

'Eighty-two at Zag!'

The haunting coded message at the 1980 Winter Olympics, alerting emergency medical crews to a potentially fatal accident at the bobsled course. Italy's 1964 silver medallist Sergio Zardini had indeed been killed while competing there in the North American championships.

Press and media

Journalists privileged enough to join their nation's Olympic squads have written some memorable Olympic one-liners. My personal favourite is *Athletic News* correspondent Fred Hatton's verdict on Jack Price (GB), who dropped out of the 1908 marathon after 15 miles, 'spent by his own folly and lack of forethought'. Hatton is run close by Arthur Daley of the *New York Times* in 1960: 'They finished no further apart than the width of a flattened sardine'.

"

'The whole publicity and what was going on in the media, really I was pretty oblivious to most of that…'

Figure skater Debi Thomas (USA), bronze medallist at the Calgary Winter Games of 1988, showing that athletes can succeed without bothering about media hype.

"

'Time: 49 and one-fifth seconds – a new Olympic record.'

This simple statement by an announcer called Harvey at St Louis in 1904 after the men's 400m, won by Harry Hillman of the USA, was the proverbial acorn from which the great oaks of timekeeping, such as Seiko or Omega, grew.

"

'Lovelock leads! Lovelock! Lovelock! Come on Jack, a hundred yards to go. Come on Jack! Come on! Lovelock wins! Five yards, six yards. He's won! Hurrah!'

Some good old-fashioned simple commentary by Paris 1924 victor in the men's 100m, Britain's Harold Abrahams on the last few metres of the men's 1500m at Berlin in 1936.

"

'I hope the Romanian doesn't get through, because I can't pronounce her bloody name.'

Allegedly from David Coleman, British commentator, at one of the many Olympic Games he covered. He thought he was off air.

"

'It's hard to take all things down, especially when the speaker has a different accent.'

American university student Nick Compton, volunteer flash-quote reporter in 2008, revealing the potential inaccuracy of such quotes.

'Afterwards, reporters searched frantically to find an Icelandic interpreter...'

...only to have Vilhjálmur Einarsson, Iceland's silver medallist in the long jump at Melbourne 1956, rescue them by reassuring them that his English was not too bad, he being a graduate of Dartmouth College, in New Hampshire.

" "

Students: 'What's it like to cover the Games?'

Ron Judd: 'You ride a lot of buses.'

Ron Judd, US sports journalist.

Spectators

Spectators are part of the 'Olympic Family' too! Where there is a crowd of onlookers, there will be noisy encouragement aimed at competitors. Roman poet, Statius, sets us down among young fans loudly cheering a long jumper 'fresh from the victory at Olympia for which the fair olive-branch shaded his brow'. In 1896 patriotic Greek spectators egged on the local boy in the first Marathon: 'Catch him, Louis! You've got to beat him! Hellas! Hellas!' And as the final stage was signalled by a cannon shot, the rumours from the suburbs fired up the crowd in the brand-new Panathenian Stadium: 'A Greek! It is a Greek! Zito [Hurrah], Louis!'

" "

'Your old philosophers beheld mankind
As mere spectators of th' Olympic games.'

The English poet Lord Byron, in his *The Deformed Transformed*. Club-footed Byron was an Olympian or even a Paralympian before his time, having swum across the Dardanelles (6.5 km, strong currents) in May 1810.

" "

'And now the Queen, to glad her sons, proclaims
By herald hawkers, high heroic games.
They summon all her race: an endless band
Pours forth, and leaves unpeopled half the land.
A motley mixture! In long wigs, in bags,
In silks, in crapes, in gaiters, and in rags.
From drawing-rooms, from colleges, from garrets,
On horse, on foot, in hack and gilded chariots...'

Eighteenth-century English poet Alexander Pope begins Book II of his *Dunciad* with this Hogarthian picture of a sporting audience.

" "

'We had to look for a leader who had a knowledge of most sports and a sympathy with all ... But we wanted more than that. In our very elaborate social system we wanted some one who could carry weight with the whole social structure in this century. We wanted a man who, if he gave his name to any undertaking, that name would be taken as a guarantee by kings and princes ... that they might grace that exhibition by their presence; and ... [that] was equally a guarantee that every humble subject of this country who had a shilling left in his pocket on Saturday, or any day of the week, might be able to spend that shilling with the certain knowledge that he would get his money's worth of true sport.'

William Hayes Fisher, Conservative MP for Fulham, and British National Skating Association president, reflects on the choice of Lord Desborough as chairman for the 1908 London Games.

" "

'All this is very pleasant but surely it lacks people.'

King Albert of the Belgians, on the disappointing turnout for the Antwerp Games of the VII Olympiad in 1920.

" "

'While he was singing, nobody was allowed to leave the amphitheatre, even for an emergency. Women gave birth to children there, it is said, and numerous people who were bored with listening and having to applaud jumped off the amphitheatre wall when no one was looking (they could not get out through the main gate as this was closed), or pretended to be dead and were carried off for burial.'

Games performance (as reported by the Roman historian Suetonius) of the emperor Nero, self-appointed Olympic victor, in AD 67.

" "

'They are like children … We have a word in French for this: *chauvinistes*.'

French Olympic swimmer and sourpuss Monique Berlioux, IOC Director from 1971 until her final rupture with IOC president Samaranch in 1985. She was referring to the American spectators at Los Angeles in 1984. Curiously, her compatriot Charles Maurras had made a similar comment about the American spectators at the first modern Games ('like overgrown children'), and even King Edward VII in London 1908 commented on their 'barbarous cries'.

" "

'The king had listened at a distance to their incomprehensible shouts and was curious to give them a critical hearing at close quarters.'

By contrast in 1896, King George I of the Hellenes had a more inquiring mind about the 'college yells' of the little group of USA supporters from far across the sea: 'Bee-Ay-Ay!' ('Boston-Athletic-Association'), 'Rah, rah, rah!' and 'Siss, boom, bah!' (both Princeton cries), plus assorted Amerindian war whoops, probably from the young crewmen on shore leave from the cruise ship *San Francisco*.

" "

'It's an incredible feeling, 110,000 people – energy at that level.'

Gabe Jennings (USA) remembers his 1500m semi-final in Sydney 2000.

'When I stood looking at the audience I didn't see them ... this is how [much] I was concentrating.'

Olga Korbut, Soviet gymnast from Belarus, won two team golds (at Munich in 1972 and Montreal in 1976) and two individual golds (floor at Munich in 1972, balance beam at Montreal in 1976).

" "

'Everything was closing in on me – the people in that huge arena, the people watching on television back home, my whole life, all those years of working and waiting. If I missed, it would be like dying.'

US decathlete Bill Toomey, preparing to start the events of the decathlon for which he won the gold medal at Mexico City in 1968.

" "

'Usually, before a race, you're concentrating on strategy, the other swimmers, the race. But at Mexico all I could think about was the twenty million people who were expecting me to win.'

Elaine Tanner (Canada), 1968 100m breaststroke silver medallist.

" "

'Then, since we are hemmed in by so great a crowd of spectators, let us strip down out of our entanglements – sin – and concentrate on running on the track marked out for us.'

Paul of Tarsus, Jewish Christian convert, missionary and martyr, *Letter to the Hebrews* 12:1.

" "

'The excitement during the race was terrific, and was made more so by the terrible noise caused by thousands of throats chanting injunctions in every language to those in front to "sit down".'

The *New York Times* correspondent, watching the Stockholm 1912 men's 800m.

" "

'The café tables [were] occupied by visitors to the Games, gasping like stranded sea robins and staring at one another in search of the stigmata of celebrity.'

The sea robin is not a bird but a fish (known in England as the gurnard). The writer was the American sports journalist A. J. Liebling, and he was commenting on the cafes of Rome in 1960, at Games-time. The visitors sitting at them and hoping to meet famous people remind one of the 'extras' in Fellini's film *La Dolce Vita*, which appeared in that same summer.

19
POLITICS

According to tradition, the earliest games at Olympia were held by the mythical King Endymion so that his sons could contest the succession to the throne – in a clear example of sport and politics becoming intertwined.

❝ ❞

'The Olympics have always been politics; the concept of sport without politics is a myth.'

French journalist François Thomazeau, writing in 2006.

❝ ❞

'We are rebels.'

De Coubertin, in his speech to the 1894 Founding Congress.

❝ ❞

'Solon: We're not interested in the limited aim of winning sporting events – only a small percentage of the athletes get that far. The point is the benefit, to the State or to the individual. You see, there's another kind of event where all model citizens get prizes – complete human happiness, and that includes personal freedom , political independence, prosperity, fame, true religion, and the safety of our loved ones.'

Lucian, *Anacharsis*. Solon, here Lucian's second-century AD mouthpiece for a political view, was historically a central figure in seventh-century BC Athens, and a forerunner of democracy.

" "

'I avoided giving the impression that I had gone [to Greece] to see the Olympic Games. At any time of political crisis that would have been a disgrace; at the present one, nothing on earth could have justified it.'

The Games of the 184th Olympiad will have been held in the high summer of 44 BC, the year in which Rome's head of state, Julius Caesar, was assassinated, on 15 March. Writing to his close friend Atticus on 19 August, the lawyer and statesman Cicero makes the assassination his reason for not travelling to Olympia. But on 28 June he had written: 'I should also like to know the date of the Olympic Games'!

" "

'Those on the sports side of newspapers were encouraged, and those with political opinions, either avoided or completely ignored.'

R. F. Church, 1948 English press official for the Games.

" "

'If only politicians had to sweat it out to get to the Olympics they might not be quite so keen to say to we sports people, "I'm sorry, you're not going".'

HRH Princess Anne, equestrian entrant at Montreal in 1976. She aligned herself with opponents of the Moscow 1980 boycott, further evidence that the British Crown is not a 'political' actor.

" "

'The Olympic Games were not revived ... merely to give contestants a chance to win medals ... and certainly not to demonstrate the superiority of one political system over another.'

Avery Brundage makes it clear in his inaugural speech as IOC president that he does not regard athletes as 'gladiators', and that the purpose of the Olympics is not to build national prestige. Elsewhere he would state that the Olympics are 'contests for individuals and not of nations.'

" "

'No one who watched the parade of six to seven thousand participants ... could have failed to be impressed. There were representatives of every race, every color, every religion, of capitalist, imperialist, fascist, communist, socialist and royalist countries, all following the same Olympic code of fair play and sportsmanship. Nothing like this has ever happened in the world before.'

Tokyo 1964, as portrayed by Avery Brundage the following year at the International Olympic Academy.

" "

'ILY'

Acronym for 'I love you'. Steve Ovett (GB), 1980 victor at 800m, caused much puzzlement when he air-wrote this message to a Russian TV camera in Moscow, for his girlfriend in Maidstone to see. Some conspiracy theorists said it was a signal in Russian; more fools they.

" "

'Some day it may be possible to look back on these Olympic Games of 1908 as having given a powerful impetus to the brotherhood of the world.'

In 1908 *The Times* was doubtful whether the claim that international athletics make for international friendship (still being plugged by IOC president Juan Antonio Samaranch decades later) constituted a conclusive argument in the Olympic Movement's favour.

'If we started to make political judgments it would be the end of the Games … What we in sport and the Olympic Movement need is the interest and support of politicians, not their interference.'

Lord Killanin, sixth president of the IOC, interviewed in 1980. Fencer Hélène Mayer (Germany, USA), Amsterdam 1932 victor and Berlin 1936 runner-up in women's foil, who had embarrassed the American Amateur Athletic Union by returning, although half-Jewish, to Nazi Germany to compete in 1936, declared: 'The Olympic Games are for international sports-men and -women, and not for politicians.'

" "

'We promise the Communist Party and the Soviet people, and you, beloved Nikita Sergeivich, that we will represent our Fatherland in the XVIIth Olympics with much honour, and will fight to strengthen friendship between athletes from all over the world.'

The Soviet delegation at Rome in 1960 addresses a collective love-letter via *Pravda* to its head of state Nikita Khrushchev.

" "

'Hitler didn't snub me. It was FDR [Franklin D. Roosevelt] who snubbed me. The President didn't even send me a telegram.'

Jesse Owens (USA) whose magnificent, loose-limbed running in the 1936 Berlin Games brought him four gold medals (100m, 200m, 4×100m relay long jump), instant world fame, and later disillusion.

" "

'I don't see any reason for anyone to say anything about abandoning the Games. War in China is nothing to do with sports.'

Jigoro Kano (Japan), founder of the sport of judo and IOC member, cynically rebuffing reporters at Alexandria in 1938.

" "

'I am most indignant at your letter dated June 1 [1958]…
[Y]ou continued your mean practice of reversing right and
wrong, wantonly slandered and threatened the Chinese
Olympic Committee … and myself, and shamelessly [*sic*] tried
to justify your reactionary acts. This fully reveals that you are
a faithful menial of the U.S. imperialists bent on serving their
plot of creating "Two Chinas"…'

Chinese IOC member Tung Shouyi in a letter to Avery Brundage
in 1958. The invective is typical of relations between China and the
West at the height of Mao's rule; in today's world of cooperation, it
seems just quaint.

Terrorism

Of an Israeli delegation of 29 (including judges and coaches) more
than a third, and six of whom athletes, were killed by terrorists at the
1972 Munich Games. Two were murdered in the Olympic Village
itself; nine were taken hostage to Munich airport and shot by their
captors during a bungled rescue operation. This dreadful deed by
Palestinian 'Black September' commandos has scarred Olympic
logistics and budgeting, especially since the rise of militant Islamic
groups in the 1990s.

" "

'We had a wide range of emotions and feelings. Early on, we
thought it might be best to call the Games off, but after some
time passed we actually thought that the Games should go on.
We did not want to give in to the terrorists. We would not give
up what we had come here to do. That was the opinion of most
of the athletes.'

Tom Hill (USA), Munich 110m hurdles bronze medallist. Dave
Hemery (GB), 400m hurdles gold medallist at Mexico City in 1968,
likewise thought that to halt the Games would have been wrong, and
that many of the athletes were strongly inclined 'not to give in to the
terrorists … We should never allow evil to triumph over good.'

" "

'Walled off in their dream world ... the aging playground directors who direct the quadrennial muscle dance, ruled that a little blood must not be allowed to interrupt play.'

This scathing attack on the 'playground directors' (the IOC) following the Munich terrorist attack comes courtesy of American journalist 'Red' Smith.

" "

'So many fatal mistakes, such negligence and such stupidity.'

Anne Spitzer, widow of murdered Israeli fencing coach André Spitzer, bitterly condemned the German handling of the crisis.

" "

'The Israeli team and its rescue was secondary to that.'

Zvi Zamir, head of the Israeli Secret Service, accused the IOC of being less concerned to rescue the abducted athletes than to shift attention away from the Olympic Village so that 'Olympic marketing' could go on undisturbed.

" "

'Of course it's an unfortunate interruption of the Olympic Games, but ... I think it will all be forgotten in a few weeks.'

Such was the bland and callous press statement of Conrad Ahlers (Germany), Chancellor Willy Brandt's press secretary.

" "

'The Games must go on, and we must continue our efforts to keep them clean, pure and honest and try to extend the sportsmanship of the athletic field into other areas.'

Avery Brundage speaking at the memorial service held in the Olympic stadium for the murdered athletes; he had declared before the 1968 Games in Mexico City that 'if participation in sports is to be stopped every time the politicians violate the laws of humanity, there will never be any international contests'.

" "

Unnamed fencer (USA): 'Should the Games continue? …
Don't ask me to decide – I'm through to the finals.'

From the *Daily Telegraph Century of Sport* (David Welch, 1999). This
must have been a member of the USA women's foil team, which was
placed equal last in the final.

" "

'After receiving his gold medal, Averbukh wept uncontrollably
while the Israeli anthem was playing in Munich's Olympic
Stadium.'

This was the European Championships (in 2002), and pole-vaulter
Alex Averbukh (Israel, formerly USSR) was his country's first ever
athletics victor in an ourdoor international athletics meeting.

20
RACIAL
DISCRIMINATION

At Mexico City in 1968, black American 200m medallists Tommie Smith and John Carlos lowered their heads in anger and raised their right arms high above their heads, fists clenched. This was immediately recognised by press and spectators alike as the formal salute of the Black Power movement. An offshoot of black Americans' struggle for civil rights in the 1960s, this movement was acutely militant between 1966 and 1972. Smith and Carlos were booed by the spectators and embraced by the media. In that turbulent summer their gesture had many times more effect than that of Czechoslovakian, Věra Čáslavská, 1968 gold medallist in gymnastics and skating, bowing her head scornfully for the Soviet anthem.

" "

'The races are of differing values, and to the essentially superior white race all the others should do fealty.'

The IOC's guiding light from 1894 to 1936, Baron de Coubertin, while preaching the doctrine of universal inclusiveness, fell well short of racial tolerance. This quote from the year 1908 is the most notorious instance, and contradicts another of his maxims, that 'racial distinctions should not play a role in sport'. He seems to have been at ease with the Nazi theory of Aryan supremacy, if not actually endorsing it.

" "

'Germans are not discriminating against Jews in their Olympic tryouts. The Jews are eliminated because they are not good enough as athletes. Why, there are not a dozen Jews in the world of Olympic calibre.'

American National Olympic Committee secretary Frederick Rubien in early 1936. Brigadier-General Charles Sherrill at once added, indefensibly and utterly falsely, that 'there never was a prominent Jewish athlete in history'.

" "

'The Olympic Code is violated every day; no guarantee of freedom is given to Jewish and Catholic athletes. This being so, our duty and that of all men of honour is to vigorously denounce Hitler's practice and to demand the transfer of the Games to another country.'

Editorial in *Le Sport*, French newspaper, 1935. In a letter to Gustavus Kirby in 1933, Avery Brundage, then president of the United States Olympic Committee, had written that the foundations of the Olympic revival would be undermined if individual countries were allowed to use class, creed or race as a reason for restricting participation.

" "

'There must be no remarks about Hélène Mayer's non-Aryan ancestry or her hopes of a gold medal at the Olympics.'

Joseph Goebbels, Hitler's minister of propoganda, in a press directive in February 1936. The foil fencer Hélène Mayer (Germany), who finished fifth at Los Angeles 1932 and was runner-up at Berlin 1936, was Jewish on her father's side.

" "

'Hey, I came here to do a job, and I did it. If you don't have a question about my race, I don't have anything more to say.'

Willie Davenport (USA), after winning the 110m hurdles in 1968 at Mexico City, in his flash quote to reporters who were interested not in him but in the Black Power movement.

" "

'Now, here I'm an Olympic champion, and they told the coach that I couldn't run. I had to stay home because of discrimination. That let me know just what the situation was. Things hadn't changed.'

John Woodruff (USA), winner of the 800m in 1936. 'They' were competition officials in Annapolis, Maryland, and discrimination against black people hadn't stopped just because of a gold medal.

" "

'I wore a black right-hand glove and Carlos wore the left-hand glove of the same pair. My raised right hand stood for the power in black America. Carlos's raised left hand stood for the unity of black America. Together they formed an arch of unity and power. The black scarf around my neck stood for black pride. The black socks with no shoes stood for black poverty in racist America. The totality of our effort was the regaining of black dignity.'

This was how Tommie Smith (gold) and John Carlos (bronze) agreed to play their medal ceremony in 1968. Smith said: 'We are black and we are proud of being black. Black America will understand what we did tonight.'

" "

American voice in audience: 'I'm sorry, but I can't take any more of this from you. Black Africa has walked out: there is no spirit of the Olympics.'

Jesse Owens: 'Little man – for that is indeed what you must be – the young people that box and fence and swim and run and shoot and do all these things for the next fifteen days have given up four years of their lives to win a gold medal. Hardly any of them will win anything but that doesn't matter. When they go back to their hamlets and villages and towns, and mothers and fathers and sweethearts and wives, they can all say one thing with great pride: "I broke bread with the rest of the world".'

Jesse Owens, at a talk before the 1976 Montreal Games. Welsh former rugby international and sports writer Cliff Morgan was present: 'The room fell as quiet as a grave. It was the most staggering thing I've ever heard.'

21
RELIGION

Is the Olympic Movement an alternative religion? Does it maybe dwarf all religions? Or – like scouting, another ethically-based movement that appeared just before the First World War – can it be happily combined with existing systems of religion?

Unexpected support for the first view comes from a terrorist, identity unknown, whom International Olympic Committee sixth president Lord Killanin quoted as calling the Games 'the most sacred ceremony of the Western world'. This is close to the idea of Baron de Coubertin, second president of the IOC and shaper of what he called 'Olympism' in the first quarter of the twentieth century: his intention (he wrote, looking back in 1936) 'from the very start of the Olympic Revival' had been 'to rekindle a religious awareness'. The second view is summed up in the words of Don Juan Antonio Samaranch y Torelló, active member in his late teens of the Fascist Falange during the Spanish Civil War, seventh IOC president in 1980, and the ruthless commercialiser of the modern Olympics. Emerging for once from his protective cover, he let slip, to his interviewer Frank Deford on US television in June 1996, the phrase: 'We [the Olympic

Movement, not the royal "we"] are more important than the Catholic Church'. You could well object that whereas, for the believer, one's religion is continuously there as a comfort, the Olympic Games, for the vast majority of the human race who are not athletes, officials and journalists, swim into view only for one month every four years.

The third view was universal at the time of the original Olympic Games in ancient Greece, and was shared by the modern Greeks, who held Olympic-type athletic contests at Eastertide, and therefore by those nineteenth-century Greeks who laid the foundations for the modern Olympics: men like the entrepreneur Evangélis Zappas, the administrator Timoleon Philemon, and the first president of the International Olympic Committee, Demetrios Vikélas.

The reader will have the satisfaction of making up her or his mind from the quotations that follow, but it is interesting that right down to the twenty-first century, individual athletes have gone into the Games strengthened and steadied by their religious convictions, and occasionally (like Eric Liddell, Paris 1924 victor at 400m, or Betty Cuthbert, Melbourne 1956 victor at 100m) with a sacred text passed to them by a well-wisher. Cuthbert's, a verse from Isaiah 40, read 'They shall mount up with wings, as eagles; they shall run, and not grow weary'.

" "

'I had the feeling that we were witnessing sacred rites being performed in an open-air cathedral.'

Sir Roger Bannister, fourth to Barthel of Luxembourg in the 1500m at Helsinki in 1952, writing of the 1948 London Games.

" "

'At certain moments, the Games had something of the religious about them.'

Franz 'Obus' Reichel (France), entrant for the 110m hurdles at Athens in 1896, and rugby gold medallist at Paris in 1900, the Games to which he refers here. His compatriot André Maurois went further and wrote : 'The true sporting spirit *always* has something of the religious spirit in it'.

" "

'There is something in the Olympics, indefinable, springing from the soul, that must be preserved.'

Chris Brasher (GB), 1956 victor in the men's 3000m steeplechase and later a sports journalist.

" "

'Poetry, music, forests, ocean, solitude – they were what developed enormous spiritual strength.'

Herb Elliott (Australia), victor of the men's 1500m at Rome 1960.

" "

'Fair or temple – sportsmen must make their choice.'

The Olympics as commerce, or as new religion? The dilemma is posed by Baron de Coubertin in his last speech as IOC president in 1925.

" "

'The Olympic movement is a 20th-century religion. Where there is no injustice of caste, of race, of family, of wealth.'

Avery Brundage, president of the IOC speaking in 1972. He saw in Olympism 'perhaps the greatest social force in the world … a revolt against 20th-century materialism'.

" "

'I guess that the message that Cerutty always gave us was "When you're out on the track, there is nobody there but you. God is not with you. I am not with you, your mum and dad are not with you".'

Australian 1500m gold medallist Herb Elliott analyses the methods of his coach, Percy Cerutty.

" "

Sebastian Coe (*looking up to the sky*): 'Perhaps somebody, somewhere, loves me after all.'

Sebastian Coe (GB) had just won the 1500m at Moscow in 1980.

" "

'I'm not Christian or Buddhist, but suddenly I felt God exists. It was crystal-clear and very beautiful.'

Japanese gymnast Koji Gushiken, telling journalists of his exaltation after his double victory, in men's all-around and rings, at Los Angeles in 1984.

" "

'God has given me the ability. The rest is up to me. Believe, believe, believe.'

Billy Mills (USA), the 'unknown' who held off all the favourites to win the men's 10,000m at Tokyo in 1984.

" "

'I believe in Allah. He is the secret of my success. He gives people talent.'

Noureddine Morceli (Algeria), winner of the 1500m at Atlanta in 1996.

" "

'The first law of Olympism as you, dear sirs, understand it is the law of moral discipline and respect for authority; the second law, a corollary of the first, is loyalty. There has to be a third … in this rush of energy there must be neither excess nor shortcoming; there must be measure. It is to the law of measure that the beauty of your sports is due.'

Cardinal Désiré-Joseph Mercier (Belgium) in his address to competitors at Antwerp 1920.

" "

'Let the statutes of the Olympic Games, which call for endurance, untiring effort, and chivalry, serve as the symbol and the fundamental idea for a new League of Nations, a world-embracing alliance, whose members, trusting in their belief in God and in their own power, will strive for mutual confidence, truth, and peace among all nations of the world.'

From a public speech at Berlin in 1936 by the distinguished Swedish explorer of Central Asia and naive tool of the Nazis, Sven Anders Hedin.

'I felt weak and as if the whole world was on my shoulders. As I walked back to make my jump, I said a prayer and asked God to give me strength and if it was all right, that I should win – that I would do my best to set a good example all the days of my life. The weight went off my shoulders and my confidence returned. I cleared the winning height on my first jump and a new Olympic record.'

Alma Richards, a member of the Mormon sect from Parowan (Utah), men's high jump victor at Stockholm in 1912.

" "

'...to have been motivated by one thing: to use my physical talents to the glory of God and the honour of womanhood...'

From a speech made in 1960 by Wilma Rudolph, the black American sprinter, on her return from winning three golds in Rome (100m, 200m, 4×100m relay). She was speaking at a banquet in her home town of Clarksville, Tennessee. There, for one of the first times in American history, blacks and whites were sitting down together at an official event.

" "

'Before each event the Americans bowed their heads and murmured a brief prayer.'

There is always scope for misinterpretation about religious practices; this Athenian reporter thought the USA pole-vaulters were praying in 1896. Actually they were blowing on their hands to keep them warm.

22
REVIVAL

The ancient Olympic Games had been discontinued in the last days of the Roman Empire, in AD 393, and the buildings at Olympia went to rack and ruin for many centuries. But the memory of the Olympic Games did not vanish, and when a knowledge of Greece became fashionable again in Europe, in the late eighteenth century, it included the Olympic ideals and texts. Meanwhile, in England and France (and even in Turkey!) various athletic meetings, with some bizarre events, had been passing themselves off as 'Olympic Games' for two centuries. However, the home of the Olympics was (and some still think should always be) Greece; and once this little modern country won its independence in 1829, there were going to be Greeks with the ambition of reviving the Olympics in their classical form.

In faraway England, from the 1840s onwards, the public school system that so much influenced the growth of organised sport was also sympathetic to Greek culture. And it was these public schools (Rugby, Harrow, Eton) and their traditions that a young Frenchman, Pierre Frédy de Coubertin visited at the age of 20 and learnt much from. Later, he discovered that in Athens, Greek industrialists had been putting on trade fairs under the title 'Olympia'. When de Coubertin, living in Paris, met a Greek lawyer, Demetrios Vikélas, living in London, and also a sports enthusiast, it was as if the ends of two live wires had been touched together. Vikélas wanted to revive the Olympic Games; de Coubertin wanted to form an international association for the promotion of his own ideas about sport education. Vikélas saw Greece as the only place to hold a modern Olympics; de Coubertin was not quite so convinced, especially when Greece went bankrupt for the first (but possibly not the last) time, in 1893. Vikélas continued lobbying energetically and skilfully, the rich Greek businessman George Averoff chipped in with a brand-new stadium, the Greek royal family showed a talent for organisation, and the first modern Olympic Games was held in Athens with surprising success from 25 March to 3 April 1896.

" "

'O leave your little passions and vain hate,
Wretches – think what this Greece of yours *has* been!
Where, tell me, where are your Olympian Games,
Where are your Panathenian contests seen?
…Her ancient place – you wise! – she shall restore
Moving towards the Great and Fine once more.
Ages to come towards ages past shall turn,
And forebears in the living be reborn.'

Modern Greek poet Panagiotis Soutsos, born at Constantinople in 1806. He proposed 'that a Games be held, along the lines of such ancient Panhellenic contests as the Olympic Games … and that it take place every year in a different Greek town.'

" "

'I conceived the Olympic idea in 1843, at the time of the [New Greek] Constitution.'

Evangelos Zappas, Greek national benefactor and industrialist, writing to Minister Rhangabes in 1857. His proposal was rejected by the Minister and the King as emotional, impractical and bordering on the grotesque. Yielding to the preference for useful arts over physical ability, Zappas compromised with a four-yearly competitive trade and industry fair at Athens, starting in 1858, and defiantly called it the 'Olympia'.

" "

'It was of his home city's well-being that the young Greek was thinking when he competed against others in racing, throwing, and wrestling. It was his city's fame that he sought to increase by his own fame. It was his city's gods to whom he dedicated the wreaths placed on his head by the Judges as a mark of honour.'

German philosopher Friedrich Nietzsche, in his early work *Homers Wettkampf* [Homer's Contest] (1872). He had never, he said, come across anyone who could inspire more respect than the ancient Greeks.

" "

'Believe me, it is worth coming to Greece for this alone … When you look down from Kronos-hill on the ruins of temple and wrestling-ground and votive monument, all these spread out at your feet as though on some huge map, you can imagine revived before you all that was great and fine in ancient Greece. The buildings crowded into the narrow vale bring back myriad memories. You recall that for a thousand years or so all the glory of Greece survived and found here its sanctification. The wreaths immortalized by Pindar float in air before your eyes. It is, so to say, a synopsis of the whole of Ancient Greece.'

The recollections of Demetrios Vikélas, who visited Olympia for the first time in 1884.

" "

'So I said yes.'

Vikélas was telling Greek students in Paris in 1895 how an invitation from the Panhellenic Gymnastic Association (of which he had never even heard) had induced him to represent it in Paris at the upcoming International Athletics Congress. His first impulse was to say no; but as he had also been asked to go by close friends, he said yes.

" "

'Mr Brookes – that warmest of philhellenes – is actively seeking for an international Olympic Festival to be held in Athens in the near future.'

A test of public opinion, in June 1881, long before de Coubertin, in the Greek newspaper *Klio*. The correspondent was evidently well informed about Dr William Penny Brookes, promoter of Olympic ideals at Much Wenlock in faraway Shropshire.

" "

'But there was no longer any need to call on memories of Greece and to seek support from the past. Sport was there for its own sake.'

Baron de Coubertin, who in 1890 was considering dumping the Greeks and banking on Brookes's British Olympic Movement.

" "

'...an inter-continental, world-embracing athletic gathering held on the antique scene and under the antique title, but modelled upon the modern form and conducted according to modern methods...'

A modern Olympics, as envisaged by the London *Morning Post* in 1895.

" "

'You need to see for yourself, but I tell you it's impossible for Athens to hold the Games.'

Harilaos Trikoupis, Greek prime minister, panicking because of the economic situation (what's new?) and trying to choke Baron de Coubertin off in 1895. Too late: for the Baron the idea of their revival was now 'not some passing fancy, but the logical outcome of a great movement'.

" "

'…as the phoenix of the Olympic Games rises again…'

The phrase used by the Greek painter Nikolas Gyzis, designer of the winners' certificate, writing to Vikélas in 1896.

" "

'You have discovered in me a wretched plagiarist of Evangelis Zappas.'

The self-proclaimed reviver of the Olympic Games, Pierre de Coubertin, writing in his hectic exchange of letters with the true reviver Demetrios Vikélas in 1896, during the run-up to the first modern Olympic Games. Evangelis Zappas, Greek national benefactor, bequethed in his will, made in 1860, funds for a celebration called *Olympia* to be held every four years. This was never fully carried out.

" "

'They envy us. Yes, they envy us … It is this modern Greece that ventures to undertake with courage the Olympic Games … all the kings and princes of the world will be asking, who are these pygmies anyway; who are these fellows who are plunged in political enmity…'

The Athens newspaper *Asty,* in 1896.

" "

Burnham: 'You ran well!'

Arthur Blake (*flippantly*): 'Oh, I am too good for Boston. I ought to go over and run the marathon at Athens, in the Olympic Games.'

(*Silence, as Burnham looks at Blake quizzically*)

Burnham: 'Would you go, if you had the chance?'

Blake: '*Would* I?!'

Arthur Blake, eventual 1896 runner-up in the 1500m, was not the only athlete to scent an offbeat opportunity. George Robertson (GB) went like a shot, though when he got to Athens, he discovered that his own discipline, hammer, was not on the programme. 'The

Greek classics were my proper academic field, so I could hardly resist a go at the Olympics'. He came third in the lawn tennis doubles, and did very badly in the discus.

" "

George I, King of the Hellenes (*sonorously*): 'I declare the opening of the first International Olympic Games in Athens. Long live the nation! Long live the Greek people!'

The King's formula for the 1896 opening ceremony became an essential part, and indeed a highlight, of every subsequent Olympics.

" "

At the risk of seeing athletics degenerate and die for a second time it became necessary to unify it and purify it. There seemed to me but one method to achieve this: to create competitions at regular periodical intervals at which representatives of all countries and all sports would be invited under the aegis of the same authority, which would impart to them a halo of grandeur and glory, that is the patronage of classical antiquity. To do this was to revive the Olympic Games: the name imposed itself: it was not even possible to find another.

Words of de Coubertin from the official 1896 Album. Now he could safely throw his weight into the scales.

The great tradition

'Certainly there is no place like it [Athens] for the holding of Olympic Games.'

Semi-official report of the Athens 1906 Games. These were inserted ('intercalated') into the standard four-yearly series (1904 … 1908), and are therefore not recognised at the official level. Nevertheless, they were successful in terms of organisation and athletic achievement and they introduced a number of permanent features such as the parade of athletes, the hoisting of flags, and the closing ceremony.

" "

'Remembering the Olympic Games: will they restore European civilization?'

Editor Dawood Barakat's headline for the Egyptian newspaper *Al-Ahram* on 7 September 1928.

" "

'Victory for eternity and universality.'

The Amsterdam medals created by Giuseppe Cassioli (Italy), who was in charge of Olympic medal design from 1928 to 1936, bore this legend (a paraphrase of an Easter hymn) on the reverse. 'Most other competitions are individual achievements, but the Olympic Games [are] something that belongs to everybody', said Scott Hamilton, men's figure skating victor at the 1984 Sarajevo Winter Games.

" "

'I could see the ancient ruins of the classical Olympic sites slowly emerge from patches of fog and the Greek temples and sculptures drift by. This was my vision of the prologue to my *Olympia*.'

Leni Riefenstahl, German filmmaker. She claimed to have made the famous 1936 documentary *Olympia* 'to celebrate athletes and to reject the theory of Aryan supremacy', though Lubovski, the Jewish boy who slashed his wrists at her cottage, would probably have disagreed. The Lithuanian-Jewish filmmaker and concentration-camp survivor Jonas Mekas said that you will find yourself mirrored in her films: if you are an idealist, you will find idealism; if a Nazi, Nazism.

" "

'Modern sport was given birth [to] in Britain in the nineteenth century, but this is no reason to think our methods are the best. Anyone watching these Olympics must be aware that a sporting revelation is upon us.'

The Times in Rome, September 1960.

" "

'Every four years … I have renewed a brief idealistic existence with this woman [the Olympic movement] who transforms pure physical effort into an experience of spiritual beauty. Now she is a raddled old tart. It is not her fault. The sceptical world has courted her too fiercely … How can one rationalise the love itself [?] It is a chemistry that makes one believe, with utter faith, that the Olympics are something much greater than sport. They are an example of men and women of all colours, creeds and races living together in harmony, striving for that supreme excellence of body and mind.'

Chris Brasher (GB) victor in the men's 3000m at Melbourne in 1956. He subsequently became a sports writer of distinction.

" "

'It is no easy thing in my country to be the son of an Olympic champion.'

Miklós Németh (Hungary) 1976 victor in the men's javelin. His father Imre Németh had been victor in the hammer throw in London 1948.

" "

Reporter: 'Did you run the race for Harold Abrahams?'

Allan Wells: 'No, this one was for Eric Liddell.'

At Paris in 1924, Harold Abrahams had famously won the 100m and Eric Liddell (GB), equally famously, the 400m. The Scot Allan Wells, 100m victor in 1980 at Moscow, might have been expected to dedicate his victory to, if anyone, his predecessor Abrahams. But he is a Scot; and so, also, was Liddell…

" "

'Now I can die without regrets.'

Sohn Kee-chung's (Korea) words after Hwang Young-cho (South Korea) had just gifted him his gold medal. To explain: the 1936 Berlin Games were endlessly harrowing for marathon victor Sohn. He ran for a country he hated; Korea had been under Japanese occupation since 1910. As a Japanese subject, Sohn was under orders from Tokyo to compete using the Kanji version of his name (Son Kitei).

Not until Barcelona 1992 did another Korean, Hwang Young-cho, win the Olympic marathon. Sohn, at that point 80 years old, was in Barcelona expressly to see the race, and had had the honour of being the final torch-bearer. Later, when the excitement had died down, Hwang invested Sohn with the newly won gold medal.

23
SEX REARS
ITS OLYMPIC HEAD

The serpent entered Baron de Coubertin's paradise through gymnastics and swimming. Australian feminist Rose Scott anticipated – correctly – that a male spectator might have mixed motives in coming to see women swimmers and divers; and their allure was to unsettle Games organisers from 1912 onwards. In the 1920s, US swimmer Johnny Weismuller, in order to show off (as swimming film star and Olympic hopeful Esther Williams or her ghostwriter delicately phrased it) his genitalia, had his Olympic swimsuits cut with the codpiece now standard issue for men's trunks.

Though the well-publicised US wrestler Kurt Angle, 1996 Olympic gold medallist, had invited athletes to join his abstinence campaign ('the best sex is no sex') in front of a volatile Canadian audience in 1999, the Olympic Village was and continues to be the focus of much vigorous international action. The CIA was even accused by Moscow's *Literaturnaia Gazeta* of forcing debilitating dalliances with young women on male Soviet athletes...

'There are some very attractive women in the Olympic Games.'

Fifth International Olympic Committee president Avery Brundage. A 1988 American TV series was entitled *King of the Olympics: the Life and Loves of Avery Brundage* and that gives you a pretty good clue.

" "

'…short-skirted and neat-legged…'

A British journalist approving of the 1906 Danish lady gymnasts.

" "

'I'd swap all the poems of Baudelaire for a female Olympic swimmer.'

The scandalous French novelist and anti-Semite, Louis-Ferdinand Céline (1894–1961), in a letter to a colleague.

" "

'Figure skating is an unlikely Olympic event but it's good television. It's sort of a combination of gymnastics and ballet. A little sexy too, which doesn't hurt.'

Andy Rooney, US radio and TV writer, on his chat show in 2010.

" "

'It wasn't that we found her [Fanny Blankers-Koen] attractive – we weren't interested in the looks of athletes in those days, it was the skill that counted.'

British speed skater Bruce Peppin, who finished 23rd in the men's 1500m of the 1948 Winter Games at St Moritz.

" "

'I got enough kisses after that goal to have satisfied a modest lady for a lifetime.'

Legendary inside-left Ferenc Puskas, scorer of Hungary's first goal against Yugoslavia in the Helsinki 1952 football final.

" "

A Tigerbelle: 'Hey Doc, if you win gold, you can have our whole relay team!'

Dave Sime (*quick as a flash*): 'Wilma?'

Dave Sime (USA) was the 100m hopeful, and Wilma was the all-desirable Wilma Rudolph, eventual winner of three gold medals at the Rome 1960 Olympics. The Tigerbelles were originally the Tennessee State University women's track-and-field programme, then by extension the USA women's team at Rome 1960.

" "

'[Morris] grabbed me in his arms, tore off my blouse, and kissed my breasts, right in the middle of the stadium, in front of a hundred thousand spectators.'

Leni Riefenstahl, of Glenn Morris (USA), victor in the Berlin 1936 decathlon.

" "

'She outshined [*sic*] other contestants with her beautiful hair, skin and attractive body, and eloquent conversation skills.'

Polish rhythmic gymnast Teresa Folga, seventh at Seoul 1988 in the women's all-around, had entered for the Miss Olympic Village beauty contest. History does not record if she won …

24
TRIUMPH
AND DISASTER

'A mighty roar [of 'Dorando!'] went up from the whole assembly as he made his way to the tail end of the procession of prize winners, and the shouts and cheers and applause and sympathy were renewed again and again. When it came to his turn to climb up the broad red-carpeted steps, placed almost exactly where he had fallen for the last time at the end of his gallant struggle, and received from the hands of England's Queen the beautiful cup, her own personal gift.'

In the fourth Olympic marathon, at London 1908, the leading runner, 22-year-old Dorando Pietri (Italy) – invariably known just by his first name – entered the stadium for the final stretch in a mental daze and a state of near physical collapse. After four times falling, rising again and continuing, Dorando was assisted over the finishing line by Jack Andrew (England) the race organiser, and the Italian flag was hoisted, even as the next runner, John Hayes (USA), crossed the line. His technical infringement cost Dorado the official victory but won him the hearts of a nation. At the closing ceremony, Queen Alexandra presented the medals to the victors. The inscription on Dorando's consolation cup read: 'For P. DORANDO / In Remembrance of the Marathon Race / From Windsor to the Stadium / From Queen Alexandra'.

" "

(*Gaston Boiteux rushes from the stands, leaps fully clothed, beret on head, into the water. He and the victor, Jean Boiteux, embrace and weep.*)

Reporters (*homing in, in various languages*): 'Coach? Manager?'

Gaston Boiteux: 'Papa!'

Gaston Boiteux, father of French swimmer Jean Boiteux, Helsinki 1952 men's 400m freestyle gold medallist.

" "

Audun Boysen: 'So, Joey, why are you crying? Are you unwell?'

Josey Barthel: 'No, I'm crying because I've won.'

Josey Barthel (Luxembourg), after winning the Helsinki 1952 men's 1500m, replies to Audun Boysen (Norway), future bronze medallist in the 1956 men's 800m.

" "

'I always said I might cry if I won, but never if I lost.'

British 1968 women's 400m bronze medallist Lilian Board.

" "

'...blind drunk, totally blotto, on top of the Olympic podium ... an asinine grin ... breathing gin fumes over the French member of the IOC...'

Chris Brasher (GB) appeared to have won the 1956 Melbourne 3000m steeplechase, but the judges' decision in his favour was postponed till the following day, by which time Brasher had had a drunken night out with some journalists.

" "

'When I walked into the dressing-room after the race … I realized in a second I had won. Somehow I had not understood it on the track. All became misty and I was crying uncontrollably. I had completely lost control of myself. I was still confused on the victory stand. Not until I put the gold medal in my pocket and grabbed it with my fingers did I finally wake up.'

Pekka Vasala (Finland) analyses his emotions after winning the Munich 1972 men's 1500m.

" "

'Nobody has milked one performance better than me and I'm damned proud of it.'

US decathlete Bruce Jenner, gold medallist at Montreal 1976.

" "

'People are always surprised when they ask me what my greatest achievement has been and I say "Coming sixth in the 1948 Olympics"!'

Macdonald Bailey (GB), bronze medallist in the 100m at Helsinki 1952, after coming sixth in the same event at London 1948. Specialists in the 100m necessarily have a very fine perception of differences, and Bailey considered his performance at London a greater achievement than the close finish at Helsinki, for technical reasons and because it was his Olympic debut.

" "

'It was a bitter-sweet moment. It was exciting to be able to win … but so sad, because I was walking away from my best buddy.'

Bruce Jenner after his Montreal 1976 decathlon victory. Jenner was deliberately separating his post-Olympic self from himself when he won his gold medals at Munich 1972 and Montreal 1976; a 'split personality'.

" "

'In order to win you must run the risk of losing.'

French skier Jean-Claude Killy, triple victor (men's slaloms, downhill) at the 1968 Winter Olympics in Grenoble.

" "

'In excellence void of risk
Among men or in hollow ship
There is no virtue.
But all the world remembers a fine deed
An achievement sweated out.'

Pindar, the Greek composer of words and music celebrating Olympic winners to order; in this case Hagesias from Syracuse in Sicily, whipping his mule-car to victory in 472 (or possibly 468) BC. He is pointing out a timeless truth, that the Olympic greats do not 'play it safe'.

" "

'I haven't seen too many American distance men on the international scene willing to take risks. I saw some US women in Barcelona willing to risk, more than men. The Kenyans risk. Steve Prefontaine risked. I risked – I went through the first half of the Tokyo race just a second off my best 5000[m] time.'

US distance runner Billy Mills, the 10,000m victor in 1964 at Tokyo. Steve Prefontaine (USA) was the iconic distance runner who held all seven nation distance records (from 2000m to 10,000m). Romanian gymnast Nadia Comăneci, thrice victor (all-around, uneven bars, beam) at Montreal in 1976, then twice victor (beam, floor) at Moscow in 1980, admitted that 'it makes [competing] a hundred times more scary because it's the Olympics'.

" "

'I chose this day of all days to run the worst race of my life.'

Sebastian Coe (GB), of his 800m at Moscow in 1980. British journalist Ken Mays wrote: 'Coe ran like a raw novice who had somehow managed to get on the track just to taste the atmosphere.' But after his victory in the Los Angeles 1500m in 1984, Coe turned towards the British press section and hollered: 'Who says I'm finished?'

" "

'Man, you no win. Bones win.'

In the London 1948 men's 100m, 'Barney' Ewell (USA), runner-up, thought, mistakenly, that he had caught Harrison 'Bones' Dillard (USA), victor, at the tape. In six words Lloyd LaBeach (Panama), third-placed, put him right, even before the photo-finish confirmed the result.

" "

'Everybody knew I was going to hit the board – except me. And then I heard this big hollow thud.'

American diver Greg Louganis, four times gold medallist (1984, 1988), famously misjudged his ninth dive at Seoul.

" "

'My God, how it hurts!'

Jim Ryun (USA) could not get over being runner-up to Kip Keino in the Mexico City 1968 men's 1500m.

" "

'My biggest loss was the Olympics. I just can't forget losing. I never will.'

Swimmer Mark Spitz (USA) to journalists, before making his Olympic 'comeback' and winning seven golds at Munich 1972. In 1968 Doug Russell (USA) had beaten him in the 100m butterfly.

" "

'They call this sport.'

Chris Brasher's (GB) bitter reflection, as the Mexico City 1968 men's 3000m steeplechase ended and Ron Clarke (Australia), who had finished sixth, lay unconscious with altitude sickness, an oxygen mask over his nose and mouth. The damage to Clarke's heart was lasting.

" "

'You are Pirie. You are dead.'

At the final curve of the Tokyo 1964 men's 5000m, in a blinding flash, Michel Jazy (France, 4th) realised that Olympic history was disastrously repeating itself: he was being overtaken by Bob Schul (USA, winner), in just the same way as Gordon Pirie (GB) had been by Vladimir Kuts (USSR) in the same event at the previous Games.

" "

'If I had landed on my skis instead of my face, it would have been a record jump.'

British athlete Eddie 'The Eagle' Edwards, last in the Calgary 1988 men's ski jump at 70m and 90m. Actually a promising skier, Edwards involuntarily joined French philosopher Baudrillard's category of athletes whose fame rests on a chronic inability to clinch victory.

The athlete dying young

A complex emotional charge attaches to any Olympian victor who dies, no matter from what cause, before his or her time. The archetype was the runner who brought the news of the defeat of the Persians to Athens in 480 BC, and the classic statement is A. E. Housman's poem 'To an Athlete Dying Young', actually published just before the first modern Games, in 1895. Familiar instances, among Olympic medallists, include Americans Ralph Rose (gold in shot put at St Louis 1904, London 1908, Stockholm 1912) and Florence Griffith-Joyner (gold in 100m, 200m, 4×100m relay, all at Seoul 1988); Kenyan's Abebe Bikila (marathon gold at Rome 1960 and Tokyo 1964); Britain's Lilian Board (400m silver at Mexico City 1968); Japan's Kōkichi Tsuburaya (marathon bronze at Tokyo 1964); and the young Israeli athletes (wrestlers Eliezer Hafin and Mark Slavin, weightlifters David Berger, Ze'ev Friedman, Yossef Romano) murdered by terrorists at Munich 1972. Dorando Pietri was twenty-two years old when he ran his legendary Marathon in 1908. A spectator cried 'For God's sake, stop him! He'll die. He's dying!', and Pietri did indeed hover between life and death for two and a half hours.

" "

'…Your command I obeyed,
Ran and raced: like stubble, some field which a fire runs through,
Was the space between city and city: two days, two nights did I burn
Over the hills, under the dales, down pits and up peaks.
…If I ran hitherto
Be sure that the rest of my journey I ran no longer, but flew.
…He flung down his shield,
Ran like fire once more; and the space 'twixt the Fennel-Field And Athens was stubble again, a field which a fire runs through.
Till in he broke: "Rejoice, we conquer!" Like wine through clay,
Joy in his blood bursting his heart, he died, the bliss!'

The narrative of the first Marathon runner, traditionally given the name Pheidippides, magnificently interpreted in 1875 by English poet Robert Browning.

" "

Patton Senior (*calmly*): 'Will the boy live?'

Doctor Murphy: 'I think he will, but can't tell.'

The Stockholm 1912 pentathlon was the first of General (as he later became) George S. Patton's many close brushes with death. He recalled: 'Once I came to I could not move or open my eyes and felt them give me a shot more hop [opium]. I feared that it would be an overdose and would kill me.' His father was, as constantly at this Games, by his side.

" "

'There is nothing worse than a woman athlete's death.'

German journalist Hubert Ostler, in 1994.

25
VOICES
OF DISSENT

Objections to the Olympic Games – and they date from the fifth century BC at least – can usually be sorted into the following categories: sheer indifference; medical, technical and psychiatric opinion; socioeconomic and political anger; and aesthetic distaste.

" "

'The origin of the cosmos, the Earth and life is a problem far more crucial than knowing who won most gold medals at the last Olympic Games.'

Norwegian author Jostein Gaarder in 1981.

" "

'By the ramparts of Olympia he celebrates his melancholy apocalypse unawares. Can we stir this mass-man, content in his Attic village, from his mindless, smug sloth? … Life seems to be measured by the feats of a victor in the throwing of the javelin, or by him who runs a certain course ten times.'

The Italian writer and literary theorist Umberto Eco. His picture, seen as if through the eyes of an ancient Greek, is of twentieth-century 'Common Man', besotted with sport.

" "

'How vainly men themselves amaze
To win the palm, the oak, the bays.'

Seventeenth-century English poet Andrew Marvell, in 'The Garden'.

" "

'Continue to chase your tails, Olympic kittens!'

Eric Dexter, a largely anonymous and untraced star, writing to the editor of *New Age* (1908).

" "

'What's hockey?'

Mahatma Gandhi had been invited by an Indian journalist to put his authority behind an appeal for funds to send the Indian Hockey Federation's team to the Los Angeles 1932 Games.

" "

'The athlete's life is absolutely contrary to the principles of good health. The way they live is, it seems to me, far more likely to produce illness than wellness.'

The influential second-century AD medical writer Galen, from Pergamum in Roman Greece.

" "

'Competition, the struggle against The Other, reveal themselves as at best infantile and at worst suicidal behaviours.'

French geneticist Albert Jacquard, in 2002. The philosopher Baudrillard called the marathon an internationally-sanctioned fetish, a narcissistic 'run to the death'.

" "

'For all the fuss made over the Olympics as a grand production, the 20th century does not, at the last, end up as Olympian. Instead, our time is more the triumph, in play, of the team and the ball over the individual and his body.'

American sports writer Frank Deford in 1996. By 2008 he had decided that 'the Olympics are yesterday's party.'

" "

'Of all the many bad things about Greece, the worst is athletes and their sort. To start with, they have no notion of good management – how should a belly-god earn enough to build up an estate? Then they cannot stand up to poverty and misfortune, as they have never learnt good manners and how to adjust to painful experience. When they are young they are superb. But when they become old, they shuffle along in shabby clothes.'

Euripides, in his play *Autolycus*, premiered in the late fifth century BC. Athletes were already notorious for their powers of consumption.

" "

'Let's Ditch the Olympics.'

Cosmopolitan headline, March 1948.

" "

'To Yossarian, the idea of pennants as prizes was absurd. No money went with them, no class privileges. Like Olympic medals and tennis trophies, all they signified was that the owner had done something of no benefit to anyone more capably than everyone else.'

The American satirist Joseph Heller, in *Catch-22* (1961), which is a novel that rejects military organisation and training, so is resolutely opposed to the competitive values of Olympic sport.

" "

'Not a farthing, not a man for the Berlin Games!'

The French Fédèration Sportive du Gauche (FSGT) in 1936.

" "

'I'm not a sports fan. I've always considered the Olympic Games a grotesque orgy of commercialism and totalitarian kitsch, closer to Soviet and Nazi rallies than ancient Greece's simple athletic games.'

American journalist Eric Margolis, son of prominent Albanian human rights campaigner Nexhmie Zaimi, in his 2008 article 'Joys of Spring in Paris'.

" "

'…the Disneyfication of the Olympics…'

Canadian sociologist Dr Gary Genosko. His savagely witty monograph *Contest* (1999) analyses atheletes' behaviour and kitsch in the contemporary Summer and Winter Games.

" "

'Much modern art … consists of … rubbish funded by various grants, and it seems the Olympics [are] to be no exception … I am going to attempt my own private cultural programme for the three hellish weeks of Olympic paralysis.'

Daily Telegraph editor Simon Heffer, in an article in October 2009, deplores the term 'Cultural Olympiad' (common to Athens 2004 and London 2012). He also objects to one of its protégés, the artist and photographer Alex Hartley, and the latter's intention, according to publicity, of 'towing an island' to Britain as part of the Cultural Olympiad. (The football-pitch-size 'island' is at present in the Arctic north of Norway and east of Greenland: watch this space.) Heffer's riposte was to apply for tickets for the 2012 Bayreuth Wagner festival, which runs concurrently. I hope he got them.

" "

'When environmentalists would bring up an issue, SLOC would say, "It's too early to do anything", and then at some point later would say, "It would have been nice, but it's too late now".'

American environmentalist Ivan Weber recalls his dealings with SLOC, the 2002 Salt Lake Winter Olympics Organising Committee.

26
WAR
AND PEACE

Anacharsis: 'Can you explain why there are no war events at the Olympic Games and the other games? Instead you give the athletes exposure ... then, if they win, an apple or a bit of wild olive?'

Solon: 'Well, these are a bigger prize than you think ... and in any case, seeing is believing – if they compete so fiercely when all that is at stake is an olive branch or an apple, what will they be like when they're fighting for their homeland and their wives and children?'

In his dialogue, *Anacharsis, or, On Physical Training*, the second-century AD Greek writer Lucian considers the relationship between peace, the Olympic Games and fighting for one's country.

" "

'The first hundred years of the Olympic Games will make clear, despite all the International Olympic Committee's protestations to the contrary, how much more the Games have served the interests of war and oppressive regimes than the interests of peace.'

French sport historian Patrick Clastres, quoted by blogger Didier Jacob, *Rebuts de Presse*, 10 April 2008.

" "

'[Gymnastics is] not unconnected with the astonishing feats of Prussia...'

Written in 1870, just after the decisive first phase, lasting a mere sixweeks, of its war in which Prussia defeated France. The 1908 Official Report would contrast 'light-hearted' recreational British gymnastics with the 'cold-blooded' gymnastics of 'more military nations', meaning principally Germany.

" "

'The efforts of all the young men of the gymnastic clubs will be in vain if their eyes are not firmly fixed on the flag, symbol of the Motherland, and symbol of all the sacrifices which France has the right to ask of her children.'

France's War Minister in 1908, Général Georges Picquart, as reported by *The Times*.

" "

'No Olympic Games will be held during the present year, or while the War lasts.'

The German Olympic Committee's release to the Associated Press on 11 April 1916.

" "

'German sport has only one task: to strengthen the character of the German people, imbuing it with the fighting spirit and steadfast camaraderie necessary for its existence.'

Joseph Goebbels, Hitler's director of propaganda for the Berlin 1936 Olympic Games as for the Second World War, quoted in the Official Report.

'I was so filled with hate, and I wouldn't ever want to be like that again.'

Heavyweight boxer Floyd Patterson (USA) won at Helsinki in 1952 by defeating Ingemar Johansson (Sweden), but at the cost of emotional corrosion. In retirement, Patterson and Johansson became good friends and ran two Stockholm marathons together.

" "

'I imagined myself shooting at enemies. Before we left, my Great Leader Kim Il-sung told us to shoot as if we were fighting our enemies. That's exactly what I did do.'

Flash quote at Munich 1972 (though he later recanted some of it) by North Korean marksman Li Ho-jun, small-bore rifle victor.

" "

'Just before curfew … the aggressors shell and burn down the Museum of the 14th Winter Olympiad. The Olympics were really something fantastic here. Now, a beautiful old building from the Austrian era and all the documentation of the Sarajevo games have been destroyed.'

Bosnian Muslim writer Kemal Bakaršić's diary entry in April 1992, in the early stages of the siege of Sarajevo.

" "

'Strike a blow in the Cold War by helping America win the Olympics.'

Fighting words from New Jersey Democrat congressman Frank Thompson in 1955. As early as 1952, the Olympic Games had become cannon fodder in the Cold War. Film star and humorist Bob Hope, to oblige Avery Brundage, appeared as anchorman in a series of Olympic 'telethons' in June 1952, saying notably: 'I guess old Joe Stalin thinks he's going to show up our soft, capitalistic Americans. We've got to cut him down to size.'

" "

'It wasn't like beating some friendly country like Australia.'

American swimmer Wally Wolf, 1948 gold medallist in men's 4x200m freestyle relay, on postwar USA vs USSR water polo.

" "

'They [the Russians] were the real enemy. You just loved to beat 'em. You just had to beat 'em. This feeling was strong down the whole team.'

Bob Mathias (USA), decathlon victor at London 1948 and again at Helsinki in 1952; later a Republican congressman.

" "

'There was some brainwashing of the athletes, as usual, and we in the Soviet team realized the responsibility we had. It was like we were coming out of the trenches and fighting fist to fist.'

Long jumper Igor Ter-Ovanesian (USSR-Ukraine) at Rome 1960. In a memo to President Eisenhower, the American Committee on Information Activities Abroad identified Russian propaganda's vital elements as not written texts, but the Sputnik satellite, the Bolshoi ballet and a Soviet victory at the Olympics.

" "

'...if Soviet troops do not fully withdraw from Afghanistan within the next month, Moscow will become an unsuitable site for a festival meant to celebrate peace and goodwill.'

US president Jimmy Carter, in a January 1980 memo to Robert Kane, president of the United States Olympic Committee. The USA boycotted the 1980 Moscow Games.

" "

'The revival of the Games will play a very important part in the lofty task of uniting the nations by consigning the barbarism of war to an evil past.'

Eminent US editor and social analyst Albert Shaw, writing in 1896.

" "

'The Olympiad leaves minor heart burnings with the representation of other nations, and altogether, while an athletic success, as a means of promoting international friendship it has been a deplorable failure.'

New York Times, July 1908.

" "

'Before 1914 [the Games] were a preparation for war; and in the event their Founder's forecast was amply justified. Today they are a preparation for peace, and also for the frightening possibilities that still lie on the horizon.'

Cardinal Désiré-Joseph Mercier, a Belgian theologian, in an article for the delayed Report on the 1920 Antwerp Games.

" "

'The lesson of the Olympic Games [is] that free competition between free men does not breed hatred but friendship, understanding, and the fulfillment of one's best effort.'

The black American sprinter Jesse Owens, whose sudden fame when he won three gold medals at the Berlin 1936 Games, and subsequent disillusionment, eventually ripened into profound insights into the Olympics. The quotation is from his autobiography (written with Paul Neimark) *The Jesse Owens Story* (1970).

" "

'The Olympics are the greatest uniting competition in the world. Every four years people come together from all over the world … They don't speak each other's languages; but, for a few weeks, they can live together peacefully.'

Fanny Blankers-Koen (Netherlands) who electrified spectators at the London 1948 Games with her no-nonsense gold medals at 100m, 200m, 80m hurdles and 4×100m team relay.

" "

'It is wonderful here, away from the bombs.'

Much of Lebanese 400m runner Zeina Mina's native Beirut lay in ruins from the Civil War as she took part in the 1984 Los Angeles Games, coming last in her heat.

" "

'When full German unification finally came in 1990, it occurred without the assistance of the International Olympic Committee.'

US sports historian Allen Guttmann, drily, in 2002.

29
WOMEN'S
EMANCIPATION

Much has changed for the better since, for nearly twelve centuries, from 776 BC to AD 393, the classical Olympic Games were governed by the local law of Elis: 'Any woman seen near, or across, the river Alpheios at the time of the Olympic Games shall be thrown off the top of Mount Typaios.'

" "

'Not womanly? No, but it's girlish, and bully for girlhood, say I. They are doing some sports out in Greece, I am told. Will Greek girls 'ave a shy? Why not? If you've been to Olympia, and seen the she-cyclists at work ... the world must make way for the Woman on Wheels!'

Lines from a witty Kiplingesque ballade, ''Arry on Spring-time and Sport', by Anglo-Irish *Punch* editor E. J. Milligan in 1896.

" "

'Even if the Committee doesn't let me compete I'll go after them just the same.'

The defiant words of Stamata Revithi, the enterprising young Greek woman and experienced runner who desired to compete in the first ever men's Olympic marathon at Athens in 1896. Official permission was refused, but she was allowed to run a full-distance marathon of her own on the following day (30 March), except that she was debarred by soldiers from completing it in the new stadium.

" "

'Women have one job and one only: to crown the victor with garlands.'

Baron de Coubertin in 1902. In 1920 he modified his position: 'Women … should not pursue records'. A glance at any French *plage* of the time should have told him he was fighting a losing battle.

" "

'Women's Olympics – unpractical, uninteresting, unaesthetic, and plain wrong.'

De Coubertin on women's participation in the Olympic Games, in 1912. In the Olympic Review of 1908 he had snobbishly asked whether sports like running and football, as played by women, would be 'a fit spectacle' for the kind of spectators whom the Olympic Games attracted.

" "

'I didn't dive for two years.'

Swimmer Velma Dunn Ploessel (USA) was just 17 when she won her Berlin 1936 silver medal in platform diving. In her first week at university, at South California, the (female) Head of Physical Exercise summoned her and 'hoped' aloud that she would not be participating in competitive sport 'because it wasn't ladylike'. Twenty-three years earlier, in a letter to the *New York Times*, Ida Schnall, captain of the New York Female Giants baseball team, had accused James Edward Sullivan, secretary of the National Olympic Committee, of what would now be called sexism: 'He has objected to my competing in diving at the Olympic Games in Sweden, because

I am a girl'. Perhaps only Sigmund Freud could fully have explained why women diving aroused so much male hostility.

" "

'We thought it was impossible to win but it was so nice to race together with the other girls. It was lovely for them to win medals too.'

Fanny Blankers-Koen after the triumph of the Netherlands women's 4×100m relay team, of which she was part, at the London 1948 Games. Avery Brundage, who was half-sure that the ancient Greeks did well to banish women from the Games, showed enthusiasm for her, as athlete and as woman. Blankers-Koen had come fifth in the high jump in the Berlin Games in 1936, where Jesse Owens gave her a signed photograph, her greatest treasure. It seemed 'impossible to win' in the relay because Blankers-Koen had arrived too late to warm-up. However 'the other girls' did get their gold medals, thanks to her spurt to overhaul their leading rival, Australia, in the final leg. She saw this as bringing joy into people's lives, and also as 'good propaganda for all women'.

" "

Emil Zátopek: 'It must have been my victory in the 5000 metres that inspired you.'

Dana Zátopková: 'Oh, really? Then go and inspire some other girl and see if she can throw a javelin fifty metres.'

Dana Zátopková had just won her gold medal in the Helsinki 1952 javelin. This was her riposte to her husband Emil in 1952, who had earlier in the same afternoon won his own gold medal in the Helsinki 5000 metres.

" "

'Eliminating women from the Olympics is a great idea. There's nothing feminine or enchanting about a girl with beads of perspiration on her alabaster brow, the result of grotesque contortions totally unsuited to female architecture.'

New York Times sports writer Arthur Daley in 1953.

" "

East German officials: 'They came to swim, not to sing.'

Answering the suggestion by swimmer Shirley Babashoff (USA) that the Montreal 1976 East German women's swimming team must have used anabolic steroids, because of their musculature and deep voices. British sports writer Sue Mott was prompted to observe the same year, in the *Daily Telegraph*, that, if we were all judged by the IOC gender-testing standard, 'there would be an awful lot of "don't knows" walking around'.

" "

'I'd like to see them have races for men and women together. If I could race against Carl Lewis and Ben Johnson, I'd run 10.2 [seconds].'

This feisty challenge was flung down by black American sprinter Florence Griffith Joyner, 'Flo-Jo', triple gold medallist in 1988 (100m, 200m and 4×100m relay), who for *Newsweek* was 'as complex and fascinating as Olympic athletes come'.

" "

'There are only two Olympic events in which make-up is part of the equipment: women's gymnastics and synchronized swimming.'

Canadian professor of sociology Gary Genosko, in 1999. On women's synchronised swimming, John Crumpacker of the *San Francisco Examiner* remarked in 1992: 'It's fine that women do it, but not in the Olympics. Give it a one-way ticket to Sea World with the barking seals where it belongs.'

28
YOUTH
AND AGE

'The great Games gave every Greek boy a strong incentive for exercise, and at the venue of the Olympic Games, Elis, ten months' preparation for them was mandatory by law. As Pindar shows, it was frequently the young, and not adults, who won the major prizes. To be like Diagoras was the fondest desire of any young male.'

The German philosopher in the Age of Enlightenment, Johann-Joachim Winckelmann, in his pioneer text on aesthetics. 'Thoughts about the imitation of Greek painting and sculpture' (1765).

❝ ❞

'...the four-yearly festival of the human springtime...'

Well-worn saying of the IOC's guru and second president, Pierre de Coubertin. It was first aired at the Parnassus Society in Athens in 1894, and there is a good example of his use of the phrase in the 1924 Official Report.

❝ ❞

'I summon the Youth of the World!'

This Berlin 1936 logo is the only one so far to have had an explicit 'message'. It quotes the words inscribed on the massive Olympic bell devised by the secretary of the organising committee for the Games of the XI Olympiad, Carl Diem. The words are difficult to read without thinking of the Hitler Youth. Diem defined sport as 'a call to the youth of the world to join together in the spirit of chivalry – a small but important contribution to ensuring peace'.

66 99

'I gave them my heart, my smile, my soul. I was playing like in the grass. I was kind like eight years old.'

Soviet-Belarusian gymnast Olga Korbut, winner of two team (1972, 1976) and two individual (1972 beam and floor) gold medals. Overnight, Korbut became a teenage star and role model. Later on she proposed what was effectively a parallel double Olympics, for under-16s: her exact words were 'to change very simple way to Olympic Games, in one competition, two different levels. Separate from, until sixteen, and after sixteen years old.'

66 99

Journalist: 'Have you any plans for retirement?'

Nadia Comăneci: 'I'm only fourteen!'

Gymnast Nadia Comăneci (Romania), after her Olympic debut at the Montreal Games in 1976, when she won three golds (all-around, uneven bars, beam) and in the second of these scored the first perfect 10 for gymnastics in Olympic history.

66 99

'I'll start shaving, I guess.'

Bob Mathias. Aged only 17 when his coach advised him to take up the decathlon, Mathias qualified for the 1948 US Olympic team less than three months later. The quotation was his answer to a journalist asking how he would celebrate his victory.

66 99

Journalist: 'Where do you go from here?'

Moulay Brahim Boutaib: 'What can you ask a flower just in bloom?'

Victor in the 10,000m in 1988 in Seoul, Moulay Brahim Boutaib (Morocco) won his gold medal just one month after his 21st birthday.

" "

'I am 26, and that is getting on for this kind of thing.'

Stephen Gawthorpe (GB), who finished fifth at Los Angeles 1984 in judo half-lightweight. By 'this kind of thing', he meant major international competitions.

" "

'I didn't make an Olympic team till I was 34.'

Distance-runner Keith Brantly (USA), 34th in the 1996 Atlanta marathon.

" "

'The first one, I was really young; the second, not very capable; the third, very injured; the fourth, old.'

US discus thrower Al Oerter, reflecting on his four Olympic gold medals (Melbourne 1956, Rome 1960, Tokyo 1964, Mexico City 1968).

" "

'As armed in bronze he won the race
to the lady Hypsipel said he
when up he went for the crown:
"That's how fast I am on my feet.
My arm and my guts are just as good.
You can see a young man go grey
Often enough before his day".'

Pindar (Olympian Cantata, iv.26–30).

" "

'It was just the thing to rouse me.'

Fanny Blankers-Koen's response to British team manager Jack Crump's assertion that she was 'over the hill'. She went on to win four gold medals at the 1948 London Games.

" "

'After my first Olympics I was just 23, and it's only now, at 43, that I'm beginning to comprehend everything.'

Where Jesse Owens had been humble, fellow American gold-medal winner Carl Lewis, at age 23, was not. One can sympathise with the sardonic comment of American long jumper Larry Myricks in 1984, that 'there's going to be some serious celebration when Carl gets beaten'. Commenting on her own maturity, Romanian gold medallist gymnast Nadia Comăneci thought similarly: 'Well, for a fourteen-year-old the Olympic Games is just a bigger competition … I'm not sure you understand fully when you're 14 how big the Olympics are'.

" "

'Can't run any further.'

Kōkichi Tsuburaya (Japan) came third in the Tokyo 1964 marathon. Nine months before the next Games, depressed, pushed and trained too hard, nursing an injured tendon, and unable to fulfil his country's expectations, he committed suicide, leaving the brief note quoted above for his mother.

" "

'…[the Italians seemed] suddenly very old…'

Greg Searle (GB), Barcelona 1992 victor, with his brother Jonathon and Garry Herbert, in the men's coxed pairs. The Italian runners-up were overtaken by them in the last hundred metres.

" "

'…like a gallant horse that had oftentimes won at the Olympics on the greatest of all fields, but now taking his rest, weakened by old age…'

The early Roman poet Ennius, quoted by Cicero.

'Triumphing over death, and chance, and thee, O time.'

John Milton (1604–1667), Londoner, pupil at St Paul's School, university entrant at age 11; visually challenged, not known to have actively engaged in any Olympic discipline except music, but wrote marathon epic *Paradise Lost* justifying the ways of God to Man. Quote, concept and mood gratefully lifted from Rose Macaulay, *The Towers of Trebizond*.

29
THE OLYMPIC HYMN

The great modern Greek poet Kostis Palamas (b.1859), who lived to celebrate his country's heroic stand during the Second World War, wrote what he himself called the Olympic Anthem early in his career, in 1895. The music was composed by Spyridon Samaras, of Corfu, seconded from Milan. The hymn was performed at the opening ceremony of the first modern Olympic Games on 25 March 1896, with a 200-strong choir behind 200 orchestral players. My own English translation overleaf was published in the Athens daily newspaper *Kathimerini* of 10 August, on the eve of the 2004 Games.

Αρχαίο πνεύμα αθάνατο, αγνέ πατέρα
Του ωραίου, του μεγάλου και τ'αληθινού,
Κατέβα, φανερώσου κι άστραψε εδώ πέρα
Στη δόξα της δικής σου γής και τ'ουρανού

Στο δρόμο και στο πάλεμο και στο λιθάρι
Στων ευγενών αγώνων λάμψε την ορμή
Και με τ'αμάραντο στεφάνωσε κλωνάρι
Και σιδερένιο πλάσε κι άξιο το κορμί.

Κάμποι, βουνά και πέλαγα φέγγουν μαζί σου
Σαν ενας λευκοπόρφυρος μέγας ναός
Και τρέχει στο ναό εδώ προσκυνητής σου
Αρχαίο πνεύμα αθάνατο, καθέ λαός.

O immortal ancient Spirit, inviolate
Father of all that is lovely, true, or great:
Come earthward; show thyself; send lightning nigh,
To robe in glory thine own land and sky.

Be it at grapple, or hurl of disk, or course,
Give lustre to the noble contest's force:
And with thy branch of olive ever fresh
Crown and make worthy and hard as iron, the flesh.

Mountain and plain and ocean with thee shine
Like some colossal white-and-porphyry shrine:
And to that shrine to worship, runs apace
(O immortal ancient Spirit) the human race.

OLYMPIC GAMES: HOST CITIES AND DATES

Classical Olympic Games

Year	Place
776 BC[1]	Olympia, Greece
772–148 BC	Olympia, Greece
144–84 BC	Olympia, Greece
80 BC	Rome, Italy
76–4 BC	Olympia, Greece
AD 1–61	Olympia, Greece
AD 67[2]	Olympia, Greece
AD 69–389	Olympia, Greece
AD 393[3]	Olympia, Greece

1 Traditional date for the start of the historical Games.
2 Postponed from 65 AD to suit the Emperor Nero.
3 Traditional date of the last Games before the Imperial ban. The dates AD 435 and at least until AD 500 have also been proposed.

Modern Olympic Games

Summer Olympics

Year	Olympiad	Place
1896	I	Athens, Greece
1900[4]	II	Paris, France
1904	III	St Louis, USA
1906[5]	–	Athens, Greece
1908	IV	London, England
1912	V	Stockholm, Sweden
1916[6]	VI	Berlin, Germany
1920	VII	Antwerp, Netherlands
1924	VIII	Paris, France
1928	IX	Amsterdam, Netherlands
1932	X	Los Angeles, California

1936	XI	Berlin, Germany
1940[7]	XII	Tokyo, Japan
1944[7]	XIII	London, England
1948	XIV	London, England
1952	XV	Helsinki, Finland
1956	XVI	Melbourne, Australia
1960	XVII	Rome, Italy
1964	XVIII	Tokyo, Japan
1968	XIX	Mexico City, Mexico
1972	XX	Munich, Germany
1976	XXI	Montreal, Canada
1980	XXII	Moscow, USSR
1984	XXIII	Los Angeles, USA
1988	XXIV	Seoul, Korea
1992	XXV	Barcelona, Spain
1996[8]	XXVI	Atlanta, USA
2000	XXVII	Sydney, Australia
2004	XXVIII	Athens, Greece
2008	XXIX	Beijing, PR China
2012	XXX	London, England

4 Added on to the Paris Exposition Universelle but not officially called the
'Olympic Games'.
5 Not officially recognised by the IOC.
6 Cancelled because of World War I.
7 Cancelled because of World War II.
8 The 'Centenary Olympics'.

Winter Olympics

The Winter Olympics are numbered starting from 1924, the First
Olympic Winter Games, rather than following the numbering of
the Summer Games.

1924	I	Chamonix, France
1928	II	St Moritz, Switzerland
1932	III	Lake Placid, USA
1936	IV	Garmisch, Germany
1940[9]	–	Tokyo, Japan
1948	V	St Moritz, Switzerland

1952	VI	Oslo, Norway
1956	VII	Cortina d'Ampezzo, Italy
1960	VIII	Squaw Valley, California
1964	IX	Innsbruck, Austria
1968	X	Grenoble, France
1972	XI	Sapporo, Hokkaidō, Japan
1976	XII	Innsbruck, Austria
1980	XIII	Lake Placid, USA
1984	XIV	Sarajevo, Bosnia, Yugoslavia
1988	XV	Calgary, Alberta, Canada
1992	XVI	Albertville, Savoie, France
1994	XVII	Lillehammer, Norway
1998	XVIII	Nagano, Honshū, Japan
2002	XIX	Salt Lake City, USA
2006	XX	Torino, Italy
2010	XXI	Vancouver, Canada

9 Cancelled because of World War II.

Paralympic Games

The Paralympic Games are now officially held in the same city as the Olympic Games, summer and winter.

Summer

1960	Rome, Italy
1964	Tokyo, Japan
1968	Tel Aviv, Israel
1972	Heidelberg, Germany
1976	Toronto, Canada
1980	Arnhem, Netherlands
1984	Stoke Mandeville, England
	New York, USA
1988	Seoul, Korea
1992	Barcelona, Spain
1996	Atlanta, USA
2000	Sydney, Australia
2004	Athens, Greece
2008	Beijing, PR China
2012	London, England

Winter

1976	Örnsköldsvik, Sweden
1980	Geilo, Hol, Norway
1984	Innsbruck, Austria
1988	Innsbruck, Austria
1992	Albertville, France
1994	Lillehammer, Norway
1998	Nagano, Japan
2002	Salt Lake City, USA
2006	Torino, Italy
2010	Vancouver, Canada

ACKNOWLEDGEMENTS

I would like to thank: Cyndy Villano and TheHivesBroadcasting Service; Mr Stephen Stuart-Smith of the Enitharmon Press; Kate Wanwimolruk and Charlotte Croft at Bloomsbury, and their texthounds Rob Hardy and Nick Ascroft; my unflappable agent Mr John Pawsey; and the Athens 2004 Olympic Games English translation team – Paul Anastas, Pauline Seale, Avgoustinos Touloupis, and half a dozen other good professionals whom it was such a pleasure to work with and preside over.

In the compiling of this book, I am particularly grateful to the following works: *Mexico 1968: A Diary of the XIXth Olympiad*, Chris Brasher (Stanley Paul 1968); *Sophie's World*, Jostein Gaarder (English translation, Phoenix 1996); *The Austerity Olympics: When the Games Came to London in 1948*, Janie Hampton (Aurum 2008); *Rome 1960: The Olympics That Changed the World*, David Maraniss (Simon & Schuster 2008); the first ten (1896–1936) of the Official or semi-official Post-Games Reports, subsequently published online by the la48 Foundation with the imprimatur of the International Olympic Committee; *The Jesse Owens Story, a Memoir*, Jesse Owens & Paul Neimark (Putnam 1970); *Punch on the Olympics* (Punch Publications 1976); *Leni: The Life and Work of Leni Riefenstahl*, Steven Bach (Knopf 2007); *The Daily Telegraph Century of Sport*, David Welch (ed) (Macmilllan 1998) and *The Complete Book of the Olympics*, David Wallechinsky (1996 edition).

I have made every effort to trace copyright for the quotations used, but there may be instances where I have, unwittingly, not succeeded in doing so.

INDEX OF PEOPLE

Abbott, M. 28
Abrahams, H. 110
Abramson, J. 25
Ahlers, C. 130
Akhwari, J. S. 34
Akritas, D. 2
Ali, M. 96
Angle, K. 3, 150
Astor, D. 17
Atticus, H. 9
Averoff, G. 142

Bailey, M. 155
de Baillet-Latour, H. 17
Baiul, O. 51
Bakaršić, K. 166
Bannister, R. 3, 25, 57, 137
Barakat, D. 147
Barnes, S. 8, 103
Barthel, J. 154
Bayi, F. 35
Bellamy, R. 57
Berlioux, M. 122
Bikila, A. 26
Biondi, M. 88
Blake, A. 145–146
Blankers-Koen, F. 52, 168, 177
Boiteux, G. 154
Boldon, A. 88
Bolopa, B. 34
Bond, D. 19, 67
Boutaib, M.B. 176
Boysen, A. 154
Bragher, C. 157
Brantly, K. 176

Brasher, C. 36, 138, 148
Bresney, B. 71
Brookes, W. P. 15
Brundage, A. 56, 86, 100, 117
Bubka, S. 25
Budd, Z. 52
Bushnell, B. 61, 86

Carlos, J. 92, 132
Carrard, F. 115
Carter, J. 167
Cecil, D. 17
Céline, L.-F. 151
Cerutty, P. 37
Chen, X. 90
Chesterton, G. K. 95
Chrysostom, D. 73
Church, R. F. 126
Clark, E. H. 60
Clastres, P. 165
Coe, S. 20, 26, 138
Coleman, D. 119
Collins, R. 61
Comăneci, N. 175
Connolly, J. B. 23
Consolini, A. 87
Cook, T. 64
Cooper, R. 9, 18
de Coubertin, P. F. 8, 116, 132
Courtney, T. 38
Cox, V. 112
Cracknell, J. 80
Cromarty, H. 16
Curry, T. 19
Cuthbert, B. 137

Daley, A. 116, 172
Davenport, W. 23, 134
Davis, W. 70, 93
Debré, J.-L. 108
Decker-Slaney, M. 76
Deford, F. 162
Deligiannis, N. 95
Didriksen, M. 29
Docherty, B. 60
Doyle, A. C. 37
Drapeau, J. 83

Ederle, G. 113–114
Edström, S. 89
Edwards, E. 71, 158
Elliot, H. 138
Enting, X. 36

Fenech, J. 75
Fick, S. 70
Fields, J. 44
Finnegan, C. 47
Flack, E. 65
Flaubert, G. 106
Folga, T. 152
Fosbury, D. 24
Franklin, N. 30
Fraser, D. 67
Freeman, C. 1, 39
Frick, X. 19

Gaarder, J. 160
Gardner, E. 81
Gawthorpe, S. 176
Gebrselassie, H. 84
Geldard, R. 68
Gemosto, G. 163, 173
Georgiadis, K. 24
Goebbels, J. 100, 133, 165
Goodhew, D. 22

Goulding, G. 53
Granger, B. 63
Grenfell, W. 16
Grey-Thompson, T. 108
Grut, T. 56
Gushiken, K. 139
Guttmann, A. 169
Gyzis, N. 145

Haig, M. A. G. 12, 59
Hajós, A. 36
Halberg, M. G. 52
Hamill, D. 75
Hamilton, S. 87
Harris, N. 112
Hary, A. 52
Hatton, F. 118
Hayes Fisher, W. 41
Hedin, A. 139
Heffer, S. 163
Heller, J. 162
Henderson, J. 111
Hicks, T. 50
Hill, T. 129
Ho-jun, L. 166
Hölderin, F. 106
Holmes, K. 5
Hunt, D. 67–68

Jacquard, A. 161
Jazy, M. 158
Jenner, B. 96, 155
Jennings, G. 49, 122
Johal, A. 84
Johnson, B. 5, 47, 69
Jones, M. 21–22
Joyner, F. G. 173
Juantorena, A. 94

Kano, S. 128

Kee-Chung, S. 38, 148
Keino, K. 79, 113
Killy, J.-C. 156
King, M. 60
Korbut, O. 123, 175
Kyle, S. 91

La Beach, L. 157
Lagat, B. K. 64
Lewis, C. 4, 49, 78, 88
Liebling, A. J. 124
Lindbergh, P. 30
Linton, L. 25
Longman, J. 30
Louganis, G. 157
Lucas, C. J. P. 70

Macadam, J. 103
MacArthur, D. 37
Mahoney, J. 99–100
Markin, V. 39
Marsh, H. 32, 78
Marvell, A. 161
Mathias, B. 167
Maughan, M. 109
Maurras, C. 92
McCafferty, I. 35
McGrath, M. 10
McIntyre, M. 39
Mercier, D.-J. 139
de Mezo, B. 43
Mikes, G. 83
Miller, S. 39, 61, 96
Milligan, E. J. 170
Mills, B. 139, 156
Mimoun. A. 66
Mimous, M. 12, 21
Mina, Z. 169
Mitchell, L. 108
Morceli, N. 2, 139

Moses, A. 63
Moussambani, E. 34
Murchison, L. 26
Mustenbrock, R. 53

Németh, M. 148
Nevala, P. 97
Newlands, P. 33
Nietzsche, F. 143
Noel-Baker, P. 92
Nurmi, P. 36, 111

O'Brien, F. 117
Oerter, A. 26, 38, 77
Ostler, H. 159
Ovelt, S. 69, 127
Owens, J. 2–3, 134–135, 168

Palamas, K. 179
Pandiangan, D. 77
Patoulidou, V. 114
Patterson, F. 166
Patton, G. 47
Payne, M. 83
Pedro, J. 87
Peppin, B. 151
Peters, J. 113
Phelps, M. 2, 76
Philemon, T. 35
Pickford, M. 38
Picquart, G. 165
Ping, L. 79
Pistorius, O. 107
Ploessel, V. D. 171
de Portela, N. S. 52
Pound, D. 5, 88, 117
Pouret, H. 8
Prefontaine, S. 86
Prieste, H. 11
Puskas, F. 151

Ramaala, H. 94
Rashwen, M. A. 46
Ratton, M. L. 3
Raven, S. 45
Redgrave, S. 4–5, 77
Redmond, J. 35
Reichel, F. 13, 137
Remigino, L. 27
Retton, M. L. 111
Revithi, S. 171
Richards, A. 12, 140
Riefenstahl, L. 56, 147
Robertson, G. S. 9
Rubien, F. 133
Rudolph, W. 111, 140
Ryan, J. 157
Ryūtarō, A. 83

Sakata, T. 79
Salumäe, E. 12
Samaranch, J. A. 15
Scherbo, V. 50
Scott, R. 150
Searle, G. 177
Shaw, A. 167
She-Jik, P. 8
Sherring, W. J. 112
Shriver, M. 108
Sime, D. 152
Smith, T. 132
Soutsos, P. 142
Spitz, M. 34, 157
Spitzer, A. 130
Stephens, H. 101
Suleymoğlu, N. 94
Sullivan, J. E. 63

Takahashi, N. 65

Tanner, E. 123
Ter-Ovanesian, I. 167
Thomas, D. 78, 119
Thomazeau, F. 125
Thompson, D. 68, 75
Thorén, P. 3
Thorpe, J. 50, 112–113
Tibball, G. 63
Tisdall, B. 113
Toomey, B. 24, 48, 123
Trikoupis, H. 144
Tsuburaya, K. 177
Tyler, D. 17, 39

Vasala, P. 155
Vikélas, D. 143–134
Virén, L. 4, 50, 75, 97
Vlasov. Y. P. 46

Wakiihuri, D. 65
Walker, J. 75
Wallechinsky, D. 65, 117
Warren, A. 67-68
Watkins, T. 106
Weber, I. 163
Weir, J. 31
Weismuller, J. 13, 150
Whitfield, M. 19
Whitney, C. 85
Williams, P. 4, 96
Winckelmann, J. 174
Wolf, W. 67, 167
Woodruff, J. 134

Zamir, Z. 130
Zappas, E. 142–143
Zátopek, E. 44, 64, 113
Zátopková, D. 66

GENERAL INDEX

Abstaining from Animal Meat 58
age 174–178
Age of Enlightenment 174
Al-Ahram 147
Amateur Boxing Association
 (ABA) 86
amateur sports 87
American Jews 99
American National Olympic
 Committee 99, 133
Amsterdam Olympics (1928)
 63
Ancient Greeks 172
Antwerp Olympics (1920) 121
archery 109
Asian Games (1994) 48
Associated Press 61, 165
Asty (newspaper) 144
Athens Olympics (1896) 68, 73
Athens Paralympics (2004) 108
Athletic News 118
Atlanta Olympics (1996) 84,
 176

Barcelona Olympics (1992) 35,
 39
Beijing Olympics (2008) 25
Berlin Olympics (1936) 33, 38
Big Issue Australia 115
Black Power movement 132
British Crown 126
British National Skating
 Association 121
British Olympic Committee 93
Brot und Wein 106

Budapest Polytechnic University
 53

Calgary Winter Olympics
 (1988) 78, 119, 158
Catch 22 162
Chines Communist Party 90
Classical Greeks 21
Cold War (1945-1991) 166
The Commonweal 99
Communism 88
Contest 163
Cosmopolitan 162
Cotswold Olympics (1821) 82
Czechoslovakia 85

Daily Mail 37
Daily Telegraph 163
Daily Telegraph Century of Sport
 131
Dartmouth College 120
The Deformed Transformed 120
disciplines 62–71
dissent 160–163
drink 58–61

endurance 32–40
England 141–142
English National Skating
 Association 41
English throwing 70
Ethiopian Herald 94

fair play 41–48
fame 49–54

fascism 98
fashion 28–31
fencing 74
Finland 93
First World War 85
flags 93
food 58–61
Founding Congress (1894) 125
France 69
France Galop 8
French Parliament 108

German European
    Championships (2002) 131
German Olympic Committee
    165
Germany 69, 99, 114
governments 92
Greece 114, 137
Grenoble Winter Olympics
    (1968) 57, 156
gymnastics 96, 111, 175
Harper's Bazaar 30
Harvard University 23
Helsinki Olympics (1952) 23,
    33, 154, 166
Herald Tribune 29, 112
Hitler Youth 101
Homers Wettkampf 143
host cities 181–184
human rights 163

In the Garden 161
Indian Hockey Federation 161
Inside the Olympics 83, 117
intellectual disability 108
International Athletics
    Congress 143
International Olympic
    Committee 43, 55, 98

Is There Anybody There? 45
Israeli Secret Service 130

Kilo 144
King of the Olympics 151

La Dolce Vita 124
Le Miroir des Sports 52
Le Sport 133
Lillehammer Winter Olympics
    (1994) 51
Literary Digest 113–114
Literaturnaia Gazeta 150
Liverpool Police Team 45
London Olympics (1908)
    16–17, 45, 153
Los Angeles Olympics (1932)
    29, 52, 75

Mammoth Book of Comic Quotes
    63
Manchester Guardian 29
marathons 64–66, 112
medals 72–80, 147
media 118–120
Medical Commission 47
Melbourne Olympics (1956)
    44, 154
Mexico City Olympics (1968)
    48, 157
Miss Olympic Village beauty
    contest 152
money 81–90
Montreal Olympics (1976) 55,
    75, 155
Morning Post 144
Moscow Winter Olympics
    (1980) 23, 35
Munich Olympics (1972) 34,
    51, 78, 155

nationalism 91-97
Nazi Germany 128
New Age 161
New York Female Giants 171
New York Times 62, 102, 123, 168
New Yorker 30
New Zealand 112
Newsweek 173

The Observer 17
Odes 68
Olympia 56
Olympia 104
Olympic Cantata 82
Olympic Code 133
Olympic Hymn 179–180
Olympic Movement 127, 136
Olympic Revival 24
Olympic revival 141–149
Olympic Village 129

Panethenian Stadium 120
Panhellenic Gymnastic Association 143
Paris Olympics (1924) 69, 93, 110
patriotism 116
peace 164-169
Persian Empire 72
politics 89, 125-131
Possibilities 107
Pravda 46
professionalism 86
Punch 70
racism 132–135
Reich Ministry of the Interior 118
religion 136–140
Roman Empire 142

Roman Greece 161
Rome Olympics (1960) 12, 29, 78
Rome Paralympics (1960) 109
Runner's World 49, 111
Russian National Olympic Handbook 89

San Francisco Examiner 173
Sarajevo Winter Olympics (1984) 87
Scotland 91
Seoul Olympics (1988) 36, 65
sex 150-152
sexism 171
South Korean Judo Association 45
Soviet Union 89
Spanish Civil War (1936–1939) 136
spectators 120–124
The Sportsman 16, 95
St Louis Olympics (1904)
St Moritz Winter Olympics (1948) 80, 151
steeplechase 78, 85, 111
Stockholm Olympics (1912) 8, 50
swimming 76
Sydney Olympics (2000) 11, 34

Taiwan 95
tennis 76
terrorism 129-131
Time 112
The Times 57, 74, 111, 165
To an Athlete Dying Young 158
Tokyo Olympics (1964) 23, 127, 156
Tous les Sports 69

Turin Olympics (2006) 30

United States Olympic
  Committee (USOC) 86
US Amateur Athletic Union
  (AAU) 29, 50
USA 63, 122

weightlifting 95
Wenlock Olympic Society 16
women 170–173
wrestling 70